The Field of Geography

General Editors: W. B. MORGAN
and J. C. PUGH

Political Geography

Political Geography

J. R. V. PRESCOTT

METHUEN & CO LTD

First published 1972 by Methuen & Co Ltd
11 New Fetter Lane, London EC4
© 1972 J. R. V. Prescott

Printed in Great Britain by
Richard Clay (The Chaucer Press) Ltd,
Bungay, Suffolk

S B N 416 07000 0 hb
S B N 416 07010 8 pb

This book is dedicated to

DOROTHY F. PRESCOTT
and
E. LEONARD ALLEN

Contents

General Editors' Preface   *page* ix

List of figures   xi

Preface   xiii

1 The content of political geography   1

2 Methods of political geographers   27

3 Frontiers and boundaries   54

4 Electoral geography   75

5 Political geography and public policy   92

References   105

Appendix: The metric system, conversion factors and symbols   115

Index   119

The Field of Geography

Progress in modern geography has brought rapid changes in course work. At the same time the considerable increase in students at colleges and universities has brought a heavy and sometimes intolerable demand on library resources. The need for cheap textbooks introducing techniques, concepts and principles in the many divisions of the subject is growing and is likely to continue to do so. Much post-school teaching is hierarchical, treating the subject at progressively more specialized levels. This series provides textbooks to serve the hierarchy and to provide therefore for a variety of needs. In consequence some of the books may appear to overlap, treating in part of similar principles or problems, but at different levels of generalization. However, it is not our intention to produce a series of exclusive works, the collection of which will provide the reader with a 'complete geography', but rather to serve the needs of today's geography students who mostly require some common general basis together with a selection of specialized studies.

Between the 'old' and the 'new' geographies there is no clear division. There is instead a wide spectrum of ideas and opinions concerning the development of teaching in geography. We hope to show something of that spectrum in the series, but necessarily its existence must create differences of treatment as between authors. There is no general series view or theme. Each book is the product of its author's opinions and must stand on its own merits.

W. B. MORGAN
J. C. PUGH
*University of London,
King's College
August 1971*

Figures

1.1   The influence of geographical factors on politics   5

1.2   The influence of political decisions and acts on geography   15

2.1   High income areas and Republican voting, Flint, Michigan, 1950 (reproduced by permission from the *Annals* of the Association of American Geographers, volume 55, 1965)   37

2.2   A list of selected features of the political landscape and other political items of interest to political geographers, which can be accurately measured   42

2.3   A list of selected topics in political geography which have been analysed by mathematical techniques   44

2.4   A list of selected topics in political geography which seem unsuitable for mathematical analysis   44

4.1a   A pattern of voting consistent with a fair distribution of electorates   78

4.1b   A pattern of voting which suggests electoral malpractice   79

5.1   The relationships between public policy and geography   97

Preface

This book has two main parts. The first part deals comprehensively with the scope of political geography and the methods which political geographers should employ. The second part deals with the three main growing points of the subject. Boundaries and frontiers, long a principal focus, are re-examined in terms of the recent trend towards behavioural analysis in geography. Electoral geography has been specially considered, because there appear to be dangers that the latest fashions in the field will distort the subject, and lead to the neglect of certain important, traditional sections. The study of public policy seemed worth special consideration since it will require detailed concern with political events and processes, often lacking in political geography, and at the same time promote contacts with geographers in other fields.

The style of the book makes one major break with tradition; there is no major historical review of the subject's literature. The decision to omit this aspect was made for two reasons. First, political geographers have shown a tendency to spend too much time looking into the past, seeking justification in the writings of Ratzel and others. This continual concern with the credentials of the subject is unhealthy and unnecessary, now that the subject is firmly established. Second, because of this tendency, there already exist many excellent reviews of the literature.

I wish to thank Professor W. B. Morgan for encouraging me to write this book and for his editorial assistance, and my wife for preparing the index.

J. R. V. PRESCOTT
University of Melbourne
Australia

1 The content of political geography

It is possible to assemble a large number of definitions of political geography published since 1954, and nearly every new book in the field adds to the collection (Pounds 1963, 1; Jackson 1964, 1; National Academy of Sciences 1965, 4; Buckholts 1966, 11–13; Kasperson and Minghi 1969, xi). None of these attempts, however, has improved on the definition of Hartshorne (1954, 178) that political geography is 'the study of the areal differences and similarities in political character as an inter-related part of the total complex of areal differences and similarities.' The main strength of this definition lies in the fact that it sets political geography in the context of all geography, not just regional geography as Kasperson and Minghi (1969, xi) suggest. It is probably salutary for some political geographers to remember at the present time that their roots lie in geography rather than political science or sociology. The further suggestion of Kasperson and Minghi (1969, xi) that since 1964 the emphasis of political geography has shifted towards analysis of the interaction of political processes and geographical area, or 'political systems', seems to refer to technique rather than subject. There has been a greater awareness by political geographers in the past decade that they must study political decisions, political actions and political forms in more detail, just as economic geographers have involved themselves with the substance of economics, and this is a view which I have persistently supported (Prescott 1959, 1965 and 1968). This greater realism in research into political geography is welcome, and is certain to benefit the subject, but the end result will predictably be an improved understanding of why there are areal variations in political character throughout the world. There is nothing in Hartshorne's definition which imposes any prescription on the technique of analysing the reasons for areal political variation, and his study of the Franco-German boundary settlement in 1871 (Hartshorne 1950), revealed a willingness on his part to undertake very detailed political analysis.

Political, economic and urban geography are the three main branches of human geography based on the prime human needs of organization, food and shelter. Any political variation between different countries, or within a single state, results from the conscious decision and action of people working individually or in groups. Political geographers are therefore concerned with the geographical consequences of these political decisions and actions, the geographical factors which were considered during the making of any decision, and the role of any geographical factors which influenced the outcome of political actions. Conversely political geographers can have no professional interest in a political decision which involved no consideration of geographical factors during its formulation, and whose implementation was uninfluenced by geographical factors and had no geographical consequences.

One point which must be stressed is that in addition to *analysing* the reciprocal relations between geography and politics, political geographers also have a duty to *describe* the areal patterns which result from them. Most geographers acknowledge that description and analysis are indissoluble sections of scientific inquiry, but the emphasis in publications dealing with political geography is on analysis. It is hard to find good, recent examples of descriptive political geography in the English language to recommend to students. Those examples which are available have been written by scholars who have worked for a long time in the field, such as East, Fisher and Spate, who have a strong sense of history and a deep interest in a major region of the earth. There is a dearth of young political geographers who think that descriptive writing is important, and therefore if it is done at all it is usually done indifferently without real application or insight. The situation is made more serious by the fact that the excellent regional geographies which are published, normally neglect the political aspects of the state, and make only brief reference, for example, to international boundaries, the arrangement of civil divisions, electoral patterns and regional alliances. This neglect of descriptive political geography will not have a serious adverse affect on contemporary scholars in the field, but the scholars a century from now will regret that so little attention was paid to this aspect. Future workers will certainly be grateful for those current publications which partially close this information gap, such as *Cartactual* and the geographical series issued by the United States Department of State.

Having reaffirmed the ideas implicit in many writings about the subject, that political geographers should analyse the reciprocal relations between geography and politics (Jones 1954; Kristof 1960; McColl 1966) and describe the political patterns which emerge from this interaction, it is now necessary to identify the actual contents of the field. There are two ways in which this task can be done. By the first it would be possible to define the contents of political geography by the topics which political geographers study. This merely requires the cataloguing of various articles and books. There are two problems associated with this method. Firstly, such a definition depends on the interests of individual scholars, and it is entirely possible that certain difficult sections of the field might be either totally ignored or only considered superficially. Secondly, the list of topics, contained within political geography would depend on the time when the catalogue was made. Thus the subject in 1910 would not have included electoral geography in which so much research is done today, and the subject in 1935 was largely innocent of the concern with decision-making which many political geographers have found a fruitful field. As indicated above, descriptive political geography would scarcely be included in the field today on the strength of contemporary studies.

The second method, which will be used here, is to construct a theoretical plan of the subject which should identify the range of topics, whether or not they have received much attention from political geographers. This theoretical examination consists of two parts. The first deals with the influence of geography on politics, the second with the reciprocal influence of political decisions and actions on geographical patterns.

The influence of geography on politics

Both political geographers and political scientists have stated that the field of political geography links geography and political science and is tilled by workers from both sides.

> I have been unable to split the hair that separates political geography from what might be called geographical politics. There must be a continuum from geography to politics, as, indeed, there must be a continuum connecting all the sciences that study man. (Jones 1954, 112)

> The subject (of political geography) is both in the fields of political science and of geography. (Weigert 1957, v)

> The bridge linking geography and political science must be built by and from both sides. (Kristof 1960, 33)

> Political geography may be defined from the disciplinary perspective of either geography or political science. (Sprout 1968, 116)

It therefore seems worth while to examine the influence of geography on politics by considering the relevance of geographical factors in the various subjects which compose political science. It is hard to find much agreement on the content of political science from the standard textbooks dealing with the subject. For this reason it was decided to use an amended form of the content suggested by the report which Robson (1954) prepared on behalf of the International Political Science

Association. The original syllabus for political science consisted of four main headings: political theory; government; parties, groups and public opinion; and international relations (Robson 1954, 183). Each of these subjects was divided into a number of subdivisions which are shown in fig. 1.1. Two other categories have been added. The first concerns area studies, political history, contemporary political questions and problems, and colonial studies, which Robson noted were taught in a varying number of political science departments throughout the world (Robson 1954, 189, 191, 201 and 203). The second amendment involves the introduction of a section entitled *linkage politics*. Among some political scientists (Farrell 1966; and Rosenau 1969) there has been growing concern with the dichotomy between students of comparative government dealing with the internal politics of the state, and students of international politics, dealing with the external relations of states.

> Systematic conceptual exploration of the flow of influences across the changing boundaries of national and international systems has yet to be undertaken and is long overdue. (Rosenau 1969, 3)

This echoes the call which some political geographers have made at intervals for an escape from the rigid division of internal and external categories of a state's political geography (Moodie 1956; Prescott 1968, 12), although this call is rejected by some political geographers who prefer the apparent simplicity and order of these two distinct sections (Schat 1969, 58). To bridge the gap between the two aspects of political science identified by Rosenau, some scholars, such as Holt and Turner (in Rosenau 1969) and Merritt (*ibid.*) are now producing specific studies which explore this area. Merritt's study of the problems of integration experienced by states with two or more separate territories and the study by Holt and Turner of the population and defence policies pursued by island states are of considerable interest to political geographers.

In fig. 1.1 geographical factors have been classified into the broad groups which represent the major divisions in the field, and an indication of the main components of each group has been provided. No attempt has been made to compile a comprehensive list of geographical factors because this must be a matter for individual taste. An examination of the political significance of topography, population size, ethnic composition and available resources will satisfy some of the traditional political geographers. Other, generally younger political geographers, seek the answer to their problems in the detailed study of human behaviour using techniques and approaches borrowed from sociology and political psychology. Crone's suggestion that 'electoral geography seems to belong more to the realm of sociology than political geography' (1967), originally seemed an overstatement which did an injustice to

	POLITICAL THEORY		GOVERNMENT						PARTIES GROUPS PUBLIC OPINION				AREA/HISTORICAL SURVEY				LINKAGE POLITICS	INTERNATIONAL RELATIONS		
	Political theory	History of political ideas	Consti- tution	National govern- ment	Regional/ Local govern- ment	Public admin- istration	Economic and social functions	Compar- ative political institutions	Political parties	Groups and associ- ations	Public opinion	Citizen parti- cipation	Area studies	Political history	Contem- porary studies	Colonial politics	LINKAGE POLITICS	Inter- national politics	International organisation and admin- istration	Inter- national law
BIOGEOGRAPHY Classes and distribution of plants	X	X	√	X	√	X	√	X	√	√	√	X	√	√	√	√	√	X	X	X
CLIMATE Types and distribution	X	X	√	X	√	X	√	X	√	√	√	X	√	√	√	√	√	√	X	√
GEOMORPHOLOGY Terrain Rivers	X	X	√	X	√	√	√	X	√	√	√	X	√	√	√	√	√	√	X	√
LOCATION	X	X	√	X	√	√	√	X	√	√	√	X	√	√	√	√	√	√	√	√
ECONOMIC GEOGRAPHY Resources Trade patterns Production (scale type and distribution)	X	X	√	X	√	√	√	X	√	√	√	X	√	√	√	√	√	√	√	√
POPULATION GEOGRAPHY Totals Distribution Quality Rate of change	X	X	√	X	√	√	√	X	√	√	√	X	√	√	√	√	√	√	√	√

X Negligible influence √ Possibly significant influence

1.1 *The influence of geographical factors on politics.*

the excellent studies by Siegfried (1947) and Goguel (1951). It has now acquired a prophetic nature as certain studies by Reynolds (1969) and Brown (1969) seem to be close to sociology. There is no reason why political geographers, like their colleagues in other parts of the field, should not seek explanations wherever they may be found. However, during such excursions they have a responsibility to ensure that no discredit is attached to the subject under whose passport they travel, through the oversimplification and careless application of techniques and approaches which experts in other areas have carefully developed. Political geographers who find the partial and qualified explanations of some of their colleagues unsatisfactory, and who search for a total explanation in related fields, should be aware that the same problems exist there, as the following quotation shows:

> It must also be recognized that limitations are imposed on the formulation of valid conclusions because the political scientist's data are often fragmentary, and never complete. Whether he has much or little, he is always aware that there are aspects of the given situation with which he deals that may not and, indeed, cannot be revealed to him. It is quite possible, for instance, to make a detailed and illuminating study of the whole process whereby an idea about public policy comes to be enacted into law. But when such a study has been completed – and by the most exacting means – the political scientist knows that his analysis has some gaps and loose ends. He cannot have accounted for all of the hundreds or thousands of persons who have exerted some influence on the legislative process; he cannot know of all the decisions made in closed committee sessions or private conferences, in and out of government, which leave no records; he cannot explain precisely how the political climate in the United States, or even in Washington, D.C., affected the legislators at this particular time; and he cannot peer into the mind of even one of the men concerned with the legislation to fathom his deepest, perhaps even unconscious, motives. From the complexity and incompleteness of his evidence, the political scientist knows there is always a possibility that the key factor in a situation is not being taken into account at all. (Hitchner and Harbold 1962, 25)

Fig. 1.1 represents the relationships between geography and politics at any particular time, the third dimension allows important historical studies of these relationships. Berry (1964) has shown that the distinction between regional and systematic geography is more apparent than real, and that generalization holds for this scheme. If the section dealing with area and historical studies is excluded it is possible to devise both systematic and regional inquiries coinciding with either the rows or the columns of the diagram. For example, a systematic study of the influence of topography on politics would select examples from a variety of situations including plains, high mountains and plateaus, and show how these features influenced, or failed to influence, the structure of the state's organization, the distribution of support for political parties and the relations between states. Alternatively a regional study would select some distinct topographic region and examine its political significance. Schweinfurth (1965) has made an admirable study of the Himalayas in this sense. Conversely a political geographer, who is primarily interested in the extent to which geography influences the constitution of states, could fashion a systematic study by examining the variety of constitutions to discover what each owes to geography. The regional counterpart of this exercise would focus on the significance of geography to the constitution of a single state or related group of states.

Before considering the relevance of geography to the aspects of politics studied by political scientists it is possible to eliminate those sections where geography seems to have no relevance. While the political philosophies of Aristotle, Bodin and Montesquieu owed something to mainly physical geographical factors, a survey of more recent developments shows that *political theories* are now formulated in an abstract situation where geography plays no role; nor can geography make a contribution to the study of *the history of political ideas*. Political scientists studying *national governments* are mainly concerned with the system which is employed. They deal with the merits and disadvantages of the executive and cabinet systems and other related topics. While geographical factors, through the operation of electoral systems, may influence the political attitudes of national governments, geography will not usually influence the administrative system by which that government does its work.

When the comparison of *political institutions* is carried on in abstract, the scholars involved will be unconcerned with geography; however, where the political institutions of specific states are compared, then geography may well play an important role. In such situations these analyses could also be classified as area studies. Finally, *citizen participation* in government and administration is not an aspect of political science which has attracted any attention from political geographers, probably for the excellent reason that geography plays no significant role here.

It is necessary now to turn to the remaining aspects of politics studied by political scientists in order to establish the ways in which geography may be relevant.

The most obvious influence of geography on a state's *constitution* will relate to selection of a federal or unitary system. The suggestion by Robinson (1961) that a federal structure is 'the most geographically expressive of all political systems' has found a response in several studies of federations by geographers. This view slightly obscures the fact that a unitary system of government may also be expressing the geographical unity of a particular territory. The study of relations between geography and federal constitutions has probably attracted more attention because of the interplay of centrifugal and centripetal factors which respectively encourage the maintenance of some measure of regional autonomy and the establishment of some central administration with limited responsibilities.

The electoral system written into most constitutions will often owe part of its character to geographical factors within the state. Those factors will mainly be concerned with the ethnic structure of the population. For example, the Lebanese requirement that there should always be a ratio of six Christian to five Moslem members of parliament, and the prerogative of the Ceylonese President to appoint representatives to parliament for minorities, can be directly related to the ethnic composition of these two states. Further, where the constitution lays down precise conditions for the delimitation of electorates, underlying geographical factors will often have played an important role. For example, the distribution of population is a main factor in encouraging those situations where rural electorates have smaller numbers of electors than urban electorates. Lastly, it is possible that geographical factors may be important in those aspects of the constitution which relate to the control of land. Geography is unlikely to play a part in situations where the constitution prohibits private ownership, although some influence may be traced to the reaction to the former control of large estates by small numbers of people. But in instances such as the land arrangements in Rhodesia and Southwest Africa there is a clear relationship between regulations and geography.

Representative studies of the relationships between geography and constitutional provisions have been made by Morton (1965), Robinson (1962) and Stevenson (1968). Morton identified the role played by population pressure and the realization of the potential of the Prairies for agriculture in encouraging the formation of a Canadian confederation in the period 1857-71. Robinson explored the relationships between geography and the federal system in Australia; and Stevenson established that there appears to be a positive association between population density and political complexity in tropical Africa.

It is convenient to consider the influence which geography might exert on those sectors of government which deal with *regional* and *local government* and *public administration* together. Firstly, geographical factors, both physical and human, are of prime importance in the generation of regional consciousness in specific areas, which frequently form the core of administrative divisions. Secondly, in cases where regional foci are evident, and in cases where the division is made mechanically, for example on the grounds of equivalent numbers of people, particular boundaries are likely to be selected in response to landscape features. Thirdly, changes in the distribution of people and in economic development are likely to create situations where local or regional administrative boundaries fashioned in earlier periods are made obsolete. Factors related to physical geography are unlikely to have great significance in this third respect. Useful studies of these aspects have been made by Richards (1965) who studied local government reform in England in terms of small towns and rural areas; by Jeans (1967) who studied territorial divisions in New South Wales in the mid-nineteenth century; by Griffith (1965) who advanced proposals for local government reform in Britain; and by Lipman (1949) who reviewed the evolution of local government areas in Britain from 1834 to 1945.

It is the second and third aspects mentioned above which will be of greatest relevance to students interested in the relationships between geography and public administration, and to these one other should be added. The centre of public administration is the national capital and geographers have traditionally made a useful contribution to the study of this feature, although few geographers today seem inclined to build on the excellent framework established long ago by Cornish (1923) and Spate (1942). Representative studies of the relationships between geography and public administration, in addition to the two already mentioned, include works by Fesler (1949), who prepared a theoretical text on the areal divisions of power, and Smith (1965) and Gilbert (1939), who both studied patterns of practical administration in Britain. The recent symposium on local government reform by James, House and Hall (1970) provides a valuable contribution to this field.

A survey of the relevant literature shows that the relationship between geography and *the economic functions* of the state have been more intensively studied than those between geography and the *social functions* of the state. The impact of such physical and human features as the distribution of resources, the nature of the terrain, the distribution of population and population growth rates on economic planning are so obvious as to require no further elaboration. A large number of valuable studies dealing with these aspects were reviewed in an earlier book (Prescott 1968, ch. 5). It is much harder to find studies of geographical influences on the social policies of states. This is not an aspect which has received any significant attention from authors of recent general texts in the field of political geography, such as Pounds (1963), de Blij (1967) and Kasperson and Minghi (1969). This neglect may occur for the very good reason that geography plays a negligible part in the development of social policies within states. The social functions of the state may usually be based on doctrinaire political theories, or the need for expediency in securing support, but studies by Scott (1955) and Brookfield and Tatham (1957) of multi-racial cities in South Africa create the impression that in these specific cases it is fruitful to examine the relationships between geography and social functions. It would probably be a useful starting point in such an investigation to assume that the inquiry could be confined to human geographical factors in situations where there were clear population sections based either on religion, wealth, nationality or race.

Turning now to the next major section which deals with *parties, groups and public opinion* an enormous variation in the interest of political geographers can be discerned. The relationships between geography and political parties forms the subject of one of the greatest growing points of the field; material is being published at a rate and in a variety of journals and languages which make it hard for any individual to comprehend. By contrast, as indicated above, geography seems remote from the subject of citizen participation which has been excluded from this discussion. While logic tells us that geography should be a factor which would merit consideration in any detailed analysis of the formation of political groups and associations, or the patterns of public opinion related to political and economic questions revealed in polls, there is no evidence that this area has been significantly explored by political geographers. One of the problems of studying measures of political opinion is that generally there is no indication of the location of the sample involved, and in any case, in countries where such polls are held, a subsequent election usually gives more precise information, within four years at the most, which can be mapped fairly precisely.

Geographers who do explore the subject of electoral geography will usually find that three themes will most frequently recur. Firstly, there is need to establish the extent to which geographical factors are involved in the designing of the electoral method; this is a subject which has already been mentioned in connection with the geographical analysis of a state's constitution. It is probable that human factors alone will be significant in this case. Secondly, where the electoral method requires the division of the state into electorates geographical factors will frequently play an important role in the selection of specific boundaries. In this situation it is likely that a blend of human and physical factors will be relevant. For example, the general limits of the electorate may be based on patterns of population distribution and ethnic composition, whereas the actual boundary site may coincide with a river or a watershed or a lake shore. Thirdly, geographical factors will be explored to discover the extent to which they account for the patterns of support accorded to each party. Human geographical factors are likely to play a direct role in this analysis, as in the identification of the Roman Catholic vote for the non-Unionist parties in Northern Ireland, or the radical farmer vote in the Netherlands (Nooij 1969). Physical factors will generally play an indirect role. Study of such features will be necessary to understand why a particular group lives in a certain area, or why people living in a specific region have a particular economic interest. In addition to these three main themes, electoral geographers may find it worthwhile to undertake research into the geographical factors which may influence a particular party to fashion political platforms which will either hold support in particular areas of strength, or capture support in areas of weakness, or the factors which may encourage a party of individual politicians to vote on a certain measure in a way which will satisfy the sectional interest of their supporters. Again it will be mainly human factors which will be involved in this analysis, although physical factors which affect forms and levels of production may also be important.

   In addition to the studies already noted the range of available work is illustrated by the following works: Pelling (1967) has written a detailed social geography of British elections at the turn of the last century; Anderson (1966) has made a micro-study of the relationships between nationality, religion and party preference in Hamilton, Ontario; Ganser (1966) has shown the relationships between social status and voting behaviour in Munich; and Blasier (1966) has demonstrated the complex interaction of economic and social characteristics, party support, and political policy in the Cauca valley of Colombia. Smith and Hart (1955), among contemporary writers, are almost alone in having examined the pattern of votes in a national assembly on regional issues. They constructed maps showing how representatives had voted in the United States' Congress on tariff issues. Similar studies have been made at the United Nations level by Russett (1967) and Friedheim (1967). One of the most detailed studies of the geographic aspects of a political group or association was made by Woolmington (1966) when he investigated the areal extent of the new state movement in northern New South Wales.

   Political scientists making general studies of particular *areas*, specific studies of the *political histories* of various states and detailed analyses of contemporary *political problems*, including those associated with *colonization*, have shown a greater awareness of the relevance of geographical factors than many of their colleagues in other branches of the subject. This is an area of political geography where there is a very close relationship between geographers and political scientists in terms of coincidence of data and similarity of approach, although there is a tendency for political scientists to underestimate the possible significance of physical geographical factors in their preoccupation with the human geographical factors. This is particularly evident in studies of the evolution of the colonial patterns by political scientists. Most attention is paid to personalities in government and the clash of interests between missionaries, traders and administrators, at the expense of identifying the significance of the availability of geographical knowledge at the particular time. The popular concept of the indiscriminate scramble for Africa is only now being modified, although detailed studies by geographers have been recording for some years that in most cases there was a genuine attempt to draw boundaries that coincided with the known patterns of tribal occupance and indigenous political organization. Another important part of this section, to which political geographers have made an important contribution, deals with the expansion of state territory, the fixing of international boundaries and the characteristics of state populations.

There is a long list of appropriate studies from which the following representative selection has been made. Zartman (1965) in reviewing the political problems associated with boundaries in north and west Africa deals mainly with aspects of inter-state relations, although he makes the useful point that boundaries based on tribal divisions are not necessarily desirable or relevant; Watt (1966) examines the political relevance of Moslem groups in east Africa and concludes that it has been underestimated; C. and B. Jelavich (1965) have written a general account of the Balkans in which the geography of that area is considered; lastly, Rose (1966) has looked at the political problems based in geography which are experienced by Australia.

While *linkage politics* is a recent development in political science the need for such an area of study has been long appreciated by political geographers. This probably results from the political geographer's greater willingness to involve himself in the assessment of the complex interaction of external and internal geographical factors. Thus the studies by Holt and Turner and Merritt (in Rosenau 1969) mentioned earlier were preceded by the studies of East (1960) dealing with landlocked states, and Pounds (1964) reviewing the historical perspective of partition.

Across the schism in political science, which students of linkage politics try to bridge, lies *international relations*, composed of *international politics, international organization and administration*, and *international law*. There has traditionally been an awareness of the relevance of geographical factors to studies in this field. Factors of plant and animal geography are rarely considered in contemporary studies, but in examinations of periods when military techniques were less well developed, the importance of understanding the main vegetation patterns was understood. It is in the consideration of international politics that the greatest investigation of geographical factors has occurred. The importance of such human and physical factors to studies of war, boundary problems, trade disagreements, secessionist movements, global strategies, power assessments and alliances has been demonstrated in a large number of studies. Typical of such works are the survey of West Germany's attitude to the Oder–Neisse line by Krippendorff (1966), the review of Anglo-German competition in Africa by Gifford and Louis (1967), a re-examination of the global views of Mackinder and Kapp by Muller-Wille (1966), and the analyses of the problem of enclaves in India and Pakistan by Karan (1966).

The importance of geographical factors in the study of international organizations and administration has not received much attention from either geographers or political scientists. It seems likely that such relevance as they have will be mainly connected with economic and defence issues. The publications by East (1968), Russett (1967) and de Blij (1967 ch. 18) are probably the best-known examples in this field. The study of international law stands between international politics and the study of international organizations in terms of the appreciation shown of the role of geographical factors. The most fruitful subjects in this sub-field have been territorial disputes, boundary disputes, the problems of minorities and the law of the sea. Further, the thoroughness associated with scholars interested in these subjects has allowed a balanced analysis of both human and physical factors where relevant. Some of the best studies in this section have been by Lord Shawcross (1967) who examined the law of the continental shelf as it applies to the North Sea, by Johnson (1966) who provided a history of the dispute between Canada and the United States of America over the Columbia River, by Emery (1967) who interpreted the question of sovereignty over the sea-bed in terms of geological structures, and Melamid (1957) who considered the political geography of the Gulf of Aqaba, an area which has created much interest among international lawyers.

While the relationships represented in fig. 1.1 occupy a single period in time, there is no conceptual difficulty in introducing a third dimension which will represent those relationships at other times. Most studies in this related field between geography and political science will involve some survey of historical antecedents, and a number may essay a projection into the future. Finally it must be pointed out that the scheme includes all levels of political organization which the geographer may wish to consider, from the international organizations at one end of the scale to subdivisions of individual states at the other.

The preparation of this half of the scheme involved scrutiny of nearly three hundred papers and books, of which only a representative selection has been recorded in the previous pages; many of the other titles are included in other parts of the book.

Three major conclusions were suggested by the survey. The most important was that political scientists have made much less contribution to the field than geographers. This is a point which is acknowledged by some political scientists.

. . . it is fair to assert that, with few exceptions, political geography has been ignored by political scientists for several decades. (Holt and Turner 1969, 200)

The second conclusion demonstrated by the research for fig. 1.1 is that analysis in this field is difficult. Only rarely was a very high degree of certainty possible in establishing the relevance of geographical factors in any particular situation. Too often the real explanation was concealed within the private thoughts, ambitions and feelings of a small number of decision-makers, or in cases of electoral analysis the countless personal experiences which have influenced the development of particular political predilections. At least in the latter situation the large number of persons concerned makes the use of proved statistical techniques appropriate where the data are available in sufficient detail.

The third conclusion is that the contributions from geographers in this area were almost exclusively by political geographers, i.e. by people who consider themselves to be political geographers, although they often have other geographical interests at the same time. This will be shown to be in marked contrast to the study of political influences on geographical patterns where the work is shared by economic, urban and cultural geographers.

The influence of political decisions and actions on geographical patterns

It is now necessary to turn to a consideration of that section of political geography which deals with the influence of political decisions and actions on geographical patterns. The scope of this field has been represented in fig. 1.2. The main geographical distributions are listed on the vertical axis. Once again there has been no attempt to produce an exhaustive list, and the subjects listed under sub-headings such as *population* and *economy* could have been multiplied many times. On the horizontal axis the first division lies between the decisions and actions of formal governments and those of other groups which will include trade unions, commercial pressure groups and rebels. Looking at the section dealing with formal governments first the second division is between overt decisions and actions. It has been thought worth while to make this distinction because in many cases the announcement of intention by a government will produce reactions among individuals and organizations which may alter existing geographical patterns. For example, the declaration by the British Government in the period

Table 1.2 — The influence of political decisions and acts on geography

Legend: ✓ Possibly significant influence ✗ Negligible influence ? Uncertain influence

	OVERT DECISIONS							OVERT ACTIONS								
	Supranational Authority		National Government			Sub-national Authority		Supranational Authority		National Government			Sub-national Authority		Non Government Bodies	
	Administrative	Development/ Defence	Administrative	Development	Defence	Administrative	Development	Administrative	Defence/ Development	Administrative	Development	Defence	Administrative	Development	Economic aims (e.g. trade unions)	Political aims (e.g. Viet Cong)
POPULATION — Distribution, Migration, Numbers, Structure	?	✓	✓	✓	✓	✓	✓	✓	✓	✓	✓	✓	✓	✓	✓	✓
ECONOMY — Production, Location, Structure	✗	✓	✓	✓	✓	✓	✓	✗	✓	✓	✓	✓	✓	✓	✓	✓
TRADE — Direction, Scale, Structure	✗	✓	✗	✓	✓	✗	✗	✗	✓	✗	✓	✓	✗	✓	✓	✓
TRANSPORT — Patterns, Type	✗	✓	✗	✓	✓	✗	✓	✗	✓	✗	✓	✓	✓	✓	?	✓
ADMINISTRATIVE DIVISIONS	✗	✓	✗	✗	✓	✗	✗	✓	?	✓	✓	✓	✓	✓	✗	✓
BOUNDARIES	✗	✗	✗	✗	✗	✗	✗	?	✗	✓	✓	✓	✓	✓	✗	✓
SETTLEMENT — Location, Size, Form	✗	?	?	✓	✓	✓	✓	✓	✓	✓	✓	✓	✓	✓	✓	✓
PHYSICAL LANDSCAPE	✗	✗	✗	✓	✗	✗	✓	✗	✓	✓	✓	✓	✗	✓	?	?

1.2 The influence of political decisions and acts on geography

before November 1965 that it would impose sanctions against Rhodesia
if the government of that country seized independence, caused a
number of firms in Rhodesia to place much larger orders for imports
while trade was unimpeded, to search for new commercial contacts in
countries which were not likely to follow Britain's lead, and to transfer
sterling funds to areas where they would remain accessible. It would be
surprising if any announcement by the United States Government that
it intended to withdraw its troops from South Vietnam, under a time-
table which seemed to endanger the security of that state, did not
result in a marked increase in the number of South Vietnamese Roman
Catholics seeking admission to other countries. The decisions and
actions of supra-national, national and sub-national authorities are
considered in terms of administration, defence and development. This
classification of government functions was developed and described in
an earlier study (Prescott 1968). In practice only national governments
exercise these three functions; supra-national authorities are normally
created for either development or defence purposes, and sub-national
authorities do not normally exercise defence functions. In this context
bilateral agreements between states are considered under the headings
of national decisions and actions. No distinction has been made between
decision and action of non-government organizations; instead differentiation is based on the main motive of the group. Firstly, there are
those groups which consider themselves to be forces for economic
change or influence; secondly, there are those groups which have both
political and economic aims. None of these threaten the integrity or
independence of the state concerned. Thirdly, there are organizations
which either seek to detach part of the existing state to form a separate
state or to join with another state, or to unite the state with another
country. These three situations are illustrated by the independence
struggle of the Kurds, by the irredentist movement of the Somali in
Ethiopia, and by the efforts of the Viet Cong to unify South and North
Vietnam.

While the plan represented in fig. 1.2 applies to a single period, it is
understood that studies will be made to show how the relationships
between decisions and actions and geographical patterns have changed
either generally or in one specific region over as long an historical span
as is found necessary. As in fig. 1.1 systematic and regional subjects
can be constructed on each axis. For example, if the subject of population patterns were of prime interest the systematic scholar could study
the varying influence of national and sub-national actions on the
distribution of population, while a regional specialist might focus on
the population movements consequent upon the actions of Balkan
governments in the first quarter of the twentieth century (see Pallis
1925). If the political geographer were interested in the influence of

development policies by national governments a systematic study might involve analysis of the role monetary policies play in altering geographical patterns. On the other hand a regional geographer might examine the influence of national plans on agriculture in West Africa (Prescott 1966).

Since this is a study in political geography it seems appropriate to examine fig. 1.2 by surveying the rows rather than the columns; the geographical patterns which are influenced rather than the political processes which exert that influence.

Population patterns form the most fluid distributions examined by political geographers. In any area the distribution, numbers, ethnic and cultural characteristics and political viewpoints of people may be subject to marked change over a short period. However, it is difficult to think of any decisions made by supra-national authorities which have caused a significant change in population patterns. The decision of the United Nations to divest South Africa of control of Southwest Africa in 1966, and the announcement by the same authority that sanctions would be imposed against Rhodesia in December 1965 could have encouraged some people to leave those countries because they feared difficult economic times, but there is no evidence that any such movement occurred on a measurable scale. It is easier to recall examples where decisions by national and sub-national authorities have probably been significant in changing population patterns. Looking first at national administrative decisions, the British Government's declaration on their support for a Jewish Homeland in the Middle East must have played a part in encouraging the migration of some Jews to Palestine; the citizenship plans announced by the Kenya Government in 1967 were probably responsible for the emigration of a number of Asians to Britain; and the official language arrangements made by the Ceylonese Government between 1958 and 1967 certainly produced a marked hardening of political opinion among the Tamil people. Examples of national development decisions which have exerted a geographical influence include the decision of the Australian Government to introduce equal pay for aboriginal stockmen, which caused a number of ranchers in the Northern Territory to switch to white workers because they thought them more reliable. The many pronouncements about the intention to 'Africanize' the economy in countries such as Zambia and Uganda must have caused some population changes. Defence decisions could influence population patterns in a number of ways. For example, the conscription plans of the Australian Government since 1963 have encouraged a number of young men, anxious to avoid service, to go adbroa until their exemption became permanent, and encouraged a number of others to seek exemption through marriage. It is easy to imagine that the announcement of support for a country, for example by the United States for South Vietnam, will cause a slackening on any flow of migrants which may exist; conversely, announcement that support will be withdrawn, as in the case of the redeployment of British troops west of Suez, may encourage population changes in numbers of particular nationals and population patterns.

Because sub-national decisions generally concern less important issues than those decided at the national level, their impact on population patterns is usually less significant. This generalization would not apply in federations where the component states or provinces had responsibility for some taxes, education and social legislation, and the conduct of elections. It is easy to imagine that legislative decisions in some of the southern states in the United States of America encouraged the dispersion of Negroes which has been evident during the twentieth century. At the level of local government the announcement of improved communications, or the declaration of intent to annex new areas to some existing municipality will sometimes initiate increased land-subdivision and rising land prices. Both these characteristics were evident in 1957 after it was announced that the Deas Tunnel would be built to connect Lulu Island and Delta across the south arm of the Fraser River south of Vancouver. The announcement of the establishment of a new port area near Tsawwassen in the same area resulted in a further rise in land prices in Beach Grove near Point Roberts.

Turning to the actions of formal authorities it is evident that their consequences are more direct and recognizable than those related to decisions. The administrative decisions of supra-national authorities which will influence population distribution will relate to the siting of headquarters; the population size and structure of cities such as The Hague and Geneva owe something to their selection for the site of the central offices of certain international organizations, such as the International Court of Justice, the International Labour Organization and the General Agreement on Trade and Tariffs. Areas selected for particular development projects, by bodies such as the Colombo Plan Organization or the World Bank of Reconstruction may undergo marked changes in the density and structure of population.

In the same way the economies of a few cities throughout the world have been vitally improved by the combined spending of military garrisons placed there by international defence organizations. In Rhodesia, South Africa and Southwest Africa the administrative actions in allocating land for the use of different racial groups is one of the most significant factors influencing population distribution and regional population structure. In a less direct way the bilingual division of Belgium into Flemish- and French-speaking areas has tended to discourage movement between the two areas, even when there was exceptional unemployment in the Borinage coalfield (Riley 1965).

Development actions by national governments have to be assessed in any analysis of population geography. Regulations governing migration, including restriction on overseas exchange transactions, attempts to decentralize industry away from conurbations, and family planning programmes are only a small selection of the government actions which may influence patterns of population movement, distribution and ethnic structure. National defence policies may be similarly important although there are fewer examples than in the case of development policies. Apart from the extreme cases of genocide there are other actions such as the relocation of villages in areas where there are some rebel activities. In early 1967 the Indian Government relocated 50,000 Mizos in a number of villages along the Aigul–Langleh road where they could be more easily 'protected' than in the hills where they normally lived; at the same time the Ethiopian Government moved a number of villages away from the Sudan–Eritrea borderland. In early 1967 the administration of French Somaliland expelled a considerable number of Somali just before the national referendum in the supposed interests of the area's security. It is difficult to think of administrative actions by local government bodies which will influence population movement or distribution although the incorporation of new urban areas or a variable rate level may produce some responses. However, many local authorities pursue development policies which offer inducements to firms and individuals in the hope of promoting a population inflow; and many also control the zoning of land for residential, recreational and manufacturing purposes which has a direct influence on the density of population in particular areas.

Since settlement patterns are based on population distribution they will be affected by the same kinds of decisions and actions. It will be generally true that actions will be much more significant than decisions, although proposals concerning changes in building regulations of zoning laws may induce a surge of speculative building which will affect the shape and size of any settlement. Administrative actions related to the selection of a capital or regional centres, and development decisions concerned with the prohibition of settlement, as in the coastal diamond fields of Southwest Africa, or the decentralization of industry to rural areas, are among the most important government actions which influence settlement patterns. Defensive actions which will influence the settlement patterns will include the relocation of population in unsettled areas, such as the concentration of Chinese in Sarawak away from the Indonesian border during the period of Confrontation; the dispersal of settlement to reduce the vulnerability to nuclear attack; and the occupation of centres in largely unoccupied territory to substantiate claims to the land and meet possible claims from other states. This last policy has been used by both the Chinese and Russian Governments during the course of friction over their common boundary.

The scale, composition and distribution of economic activities are sensitive to official decisions and actions; administrative decisions by supra-national authorities and all categories of decisions by national and sub-national authorities may have economic implications. In some cases announcements of future policy will halt the decline in a particular industry; promises of support for the dairy industry by Australian federal and state governments in 1965 reduced the pressure on uneconomic farmers to leave the industry; such farmers were persuaded to continue until the promised improved subsidies became available. In some cases announced policies may stimulate economic activity. The resolutions condemning South Africa in the United Nations and the economic sanctions supported in that assembly have been one of the factors fostering the search for oilfields in South Africa's territory and continental shelf. Lastly the proposals for nationalization announced by President Nyerere, at Arusha in 1967, resulted in a marked decline in the investment in the nominated activities and similar industries. This has led to reduced efficiency as machinery was not maintained according to usual standards. Similarly, without creating legislation, the Canadian and Australian Governments have been able to discourage wheat production by drawing attention to the overproduction throughout the world and indicating that they will be unable to maintain former price levels in these circumstances. The consequences of official decisions for economic geography do not seem to have attracted much attention in the available literature; by contrast many studies are available to show the consequence of official actions on economic patterns. In a symposium on the law of the sea (Alexander 1967), Christy and Chapman discussed the significance of international decisions on fishing industries throughout the world, and Bascom studied the effect of similar agreements on undersea mining. Examples of the influence of national administrative actions on economic patterns have been provided by Breton (1968) who studied the geographical results of the creation of the Punjab and Haryana States in India, and Moseley (1965) who examined the economic development which had occurred in various parts of China following the creation of national minority areas. In the field of national and sub-national development actions there is a wealth of literature, much of which has been surveyed in an earlier study (Prescott 1968, ch. 5). Some useful papers not contained in that list include the analysis by Stephenson (1968) of actions by the Pakistan Government in the economic field; the description by Gvelesiani (1965) of government influence on the location and scale of industry in the Georgian Soviet Socialist Republic; and the survey by Zwanzig (1965) of the economic significance of nature conservation regulations in central Europe. By contrast although national defence policies may have an important effect on economic patterns through the strategic location of industries, through stockpiling and through the use of blockades as a military weapon little attention has been given to the subject. The recent paper by Zimmerman and Klingemann (1967) is exceptional. They investigated the hypothesis that the enormous funds expended on defence contracts played a significant role in promoting the disproportionate development of the main industrial regions of West Germany. They concluded that underdeveloped areas and designated regional growth points derived little benefit from defence programmes; that the defence spending in the Ruhr was not a major factor in that region's economy, and that the Rhine–Main and Munich areas seemed to derive most benefit.

International trade produces a specialized economic pattern which seems largely unaffected by administrative decisions and actions at all three levels of government; nor does it seem likely that sub-national development decisions will very often play a significant role in influencing either the direction, or scale, or composition of trade patterns. Announcements by supra-national and national authorities concerning development proposals can sometimes be relevant. The flow of funds from one currency to another clearly reacted to the statements by the International Monetary Fund and some national governments during the major European currency crises in 1967 and 1968. Statements regarding the intention to avoid devaluation or revaluation are less significant because no government would publicly anticipate these particular monetary policies. The proposals for certain commodity agreements may influence trade patterns in the items concerned either when the agreement is being concluded, or when it appears to be running into difficulties. The withholding of Japanese wheat orders during June 1969, which was a difficult time for members of the International Wheat Agreement, illustrates this point. The development actions of sub-national authorities are less important in altering trade patterns unless the component states in a federation have the authority to negotiate agreements with foreign countries within the general tariff structure of the whole country. For example, it is now almost an annual tradition for the Premier of Victoria in Australia to tour European and North American states in search of valuable commercial contacts which will benefit Victoria. Similar journeys are also undertaken by officials of British Columbia and Quebec in the Canadian federation. The greatest influence of supra-national authorities on trade patterns is exerted by those which are concerned with the provision of foreign aid or the regulation of tariff levels. However, these organizations exert a much smaller influence than the combined actions of national governments.

A great deal of international commodity movement can be explained by reference to tariff levels, subsidies and differential freight rates which are set by sovereign states. In September and October 1969 the continued export of Canadian wheat to China was entirely explained by a Canadian Government decision to negotiate with striking wharf labourers for exemption for this commodity; thus wheat continued to leave Vancouver at a time when exports from British Columbia were trapped in the Province. The defence policies mentioned above, such as stockpiling and sanctions will also produce direct affects on trade patterns, as the excellent study by Hurstfield (1953) showed in the case of the United Kingdom.

Territorial patterns of authority are rarely influenced directly by decisions at any level of government; usually it requires an official action. In some cases there may be a defensive reaction to threats by individual states or groups of states. For example, the rearrangement of territorial authority in the Middle East in June 1967 may be said to be partially a consequence of Israeli reaction to Arab statements of intention to eliminate the political existence of Israel. But normally there are also actions at the same time which may be more decisive in provoking the reaction.

With the exception of supra-national development and defence actions patterns of territorial authority may be altered by a number of government actions. For example, the administrative arrangements made by the League of Nations and its successor, the United Nations, in respect of such areas as Eritrea, Tanganyika and Rwanda-Urundi, and Kamerun are most important in explaining the patterns which exist there today. National and sub-national administrative and development actions are generally responsible for the different patterns of local government areas, electorates and special planning regions, which have been used in some areas over a protracted period.

National defence actions which will alter boundaries and patterns of authority will be mainly concerned with international boundaries. The acquisition of strategic colonies, such as Gibraltar; the relinquishing of colonies which have become a liability such as Aden; the creation of buffer states as in the case of the Wakhan strip in Afghanistan; the elimination of dangerous salients as in the case of Greek claims against Bulgaria at Versailles; the conquest of territory giving access to the sea, as in the case of Israel and the Gulf of Aqaba, are all examples of defence actions which create new patterns of authority and, with the exception of decolonization, new international boundaries. Internal re-organization to fulfil defence motives will usually relate to secessionist movements which have been defeated. In such cases successful governments will often change the internal boundaries to reduce the regional identity of such movements, for example, the names of Buganda,

Katanga and Barotseland disappeared from the African map during the period 1964–9, and the first two areas were reshaped.

In recent years there has been a growing awareness that the regulations imposed by governments which govern private actions and the actions of government departments may influence the nature of the physical landscape, especially in terms of vegetation and soil erosion. Simple decisions are only likely to have an effect at the national and sub-national level, where they may encourage or discourage development of areas in the light of proposed new regulations, which may relate to forest clearing or foreshore development. Administrative actions are unlikely to influence the nature of the physical landscape but development policies and defence policies may be very important in this respect. For example, the opening of new areas to settlement will often cause major vegetation changes. The provision of various recreational sites around Vancouver has required the clearing of many acres of forest, and the development of irrigation areas in the Riverina of Australia, has transformed the landscape appearance which now has a much lower density of trees than before. Conversely reafforestation programmes in Israel and parts of the Tennessee valley have changed those landscapes, and conservation programmes in the Transkei have removed traces of serious gully erosion from many areas. In many parts of the world mining ventures have changed both the topography and vegetation of areas where open-cast methods are used; and too often the piecemeal development of shorelines has resulted in some harbours being seriously silted and some beaches being swept away. If the fish and fauna of any area are included as part of the physical landscape, then their distribution has generally been severely affected by the growth of urban areas. Defence policies produce a smaller total effect but in certain areas, such as South Vietnam, defoliation by chemicals, or the withdrawal of maintenance from plantations has resulted in vegetation changes.

Most governments throughout the world prescribe fairly comprehensive regulations to control the conduct of the transport industry, and national or local governments are normally responsible for the provision of public highways. The decisions of supra-national authorities and their administrative actions rarely exert any influence on transport patterns, although belligerent statements by the Arab League against Israel, or the United Nations General Assembly against Rhodesia or South Africa may induce those countries to take certain steps to improve the variety of transport links available for strategic raw materials. The defence and development actions of all three levels of government have a profound influence on the transport pattern which evolves. The co-operation of Asian states, Burma excepted, to build the Asian Highway has increased the volume of road traffic between Europe and Asia; the nationalization of railways in Britain has ultimately produced major changes in the pattern of services available; the legislation by many governments against road haulage has enabled railways to survive in what are apparently uneconomic situations. The very interesting book by Wolfe (1963) remains the best study in this general field; more recently Helin (1968) has shown how the Pakistan Government has subsidized shipping and air companies to facilitate communications between the two parts of the state.

It is now necessary to consider the geographical significance of actions by non-government groups. They could be classified in a number of different ways. For example, they could be classified according to their aims. Some of these organizations or pressure groups are primarily concerned with economic matters, such as higher wages, price stability, or agricultural subsidies and tariff levels for manufactured imports. Others may be concerned solely with social reform or educational standards; and still others may aim at political changes involving electoral systems or the state's foreign policy. The problem of this classification is that it would not produce exclusive categories; many groups now have a broad set of primary aims. For example, the trade unions in Britain and Australia, originally formed for economic reform and protection now are deeply involved in the total political process. These non-government associations could also be classified by the methods they employ to secure their objectives. Some will employ only constitutional methods, some will use economic sanctions and others will wage total war against the state. In fact, there is no single classification which will satisfy all geographers who are interested in this subject, and each should obviously use that which is most appropriate to the particular research project concerned. In this case it is considered sufficient to make a broad distinction between those groups who promote change or the conservation of the existing, economic, social and political system within the existing state territory, and those who seek changes, usually political, which involve some alteration in the state's area. For example, the changes proposed by the most radical trade unions in Australia do not involve any change in the area of the state; on the other hand, the changes proposed by the rebels in the Nigerian civil war, or by the political leaders of the Somali in Ethiopia, or by the Viet Cong in South Vietnam involved changes in the state area. If such movements succeeded, Nigeria's territory would have been reduced by the formation of an independent Biafra; the Haud and Ogaden of Ethiopia would be detached to join the Somali Republic; and the whole of South Vietnam would be merged with North Vietnam.

Looking first at those groups which operate without intention to change the territorial sovereignty of the state, it is probable that their most important influences will be exerted through reactions by the government. Thus the economic agitation by dairy farmers in Australia is important because of the contribution which it makes to government decisions to limit the production of margarine and continue favourable marketing arrangements for butter exports; the importance of the movement for Sikh autonomy in the Punjab is now seen through the creation of a separate state by the Indian Government to satisfy this demand. These activities by non-government organizations may influence any type of geographical pattern. Influences on the economic and administrative patterns have already been mentioned. The flow of international trade may be influenced by dock strikes; labour organizations may resist the establishment of new handling techniques at ports, as illustrated by the decision of an Anglo-Australian company to locate its container terminal in Europe rather than at London because of labour unrest; and agitation by various groups may prevent the government from closing down certain rail services. While international boundaries are unlikely to be affected by such activities, many governments have taken local sympathies into account in constructing patterns of local administration. Where the physical landscape is concerned it is usual for the pressure to be in favour of maintaining a certain area in its natural state. Thus the Victorian State Government faced strong public opposition when it announced plans to create a number of farms in the Little Desert of western Victoria; the opponents of the scheme included botanists, bird watchers, rambling clubs and agricultural economists.

While some of the geographical significance of other groups will lie in the reaction which they provoke from the government, they are also likely to have a more direct influence on the landscape and geographical patterns. For example, the civil war in Nigeria had a direct influence on the distribution of population; on the temporary dislocation of oil production in the Niger Delta; on the stimulation of groundnut production in the Northern Region to replace lost revenue from declining exports of palm kernels; on the pattern of regional government; and on the communication networks in the country. The north–south route which terminates at Port Harcourt was out of operation during the civil war, and imports of fuel oil into Chad, which formerly went via the Niger and Benue rivers, were taken overland via Pointe Noire in Congo Brazzaville during the war. If such secessionist movements are successful, then new international boundaries are likely to result; if they fail, then the governments concerned will make such arrangements as they can to ensure that the problem does not arise again, either by making concessions to local feelings or by transferring sections of the population.

The particular study of the geographical significance of secessionist and rebel movements has not received much attention; the most comprehensive accounts have been provided by McColl (1967 and 1969) and Prescott (1968, 59–72).

There are two points which stand out in this inventory of the influence of political decisions and actions on geographical patterns. Firstly, it is evident that this aspect of political geography attracts less interdisciplinary study. Lawyers, historians and particularly political scientists, whose contributions were recognized in tracing the significance of geographical factors for political events, are largely absent from this reciprocal study. With few exceptions, economists alone share the dual interest of the political geographer. By contrast, the political geographer is joined in this study by other geographers who were not represented in the analysis of geographical influences on politics. Geographers who make detailed studies of economics, demography, transport, urban patterns and ecology cannot afford to neglect the influence of government regulations and the action of non-government pressure groups in making their study. Some of these scholars may be shocked at the breadth of the claim for political geography advanced here, but this initial reaction will generally give way to the realization that the overlapping of political geography with other fields merely cements the unity of the subject. What is important is not whether, for example, a political geographer or an urban geographer studies the formation, form and function of capitals, but that this subject should be studied by some geographer, who should be aware that other geographers with other interests may have approached the subject from another viewpoint.

The only firm 'territorial claim' which is made in respect of both major aspects of political geography is that military geography is a subfield of the larger subject. This claim has been made before (Wright 1944, 193–3; Prescott 1968, 102–3), and rests on the fact that military policies form a continuum with other administrative and economic policies designed to strengthen the state and weaken potential enemies and that war or preparation for war can have profound effects on the distribution of population, the delimitation of international boundaries, and the development of new resources and trading contacts.

The second major point is that it is much easier to establish a causal relation between government actions and altered geographical patterns than it is to establish a similar relation between geographical factors and the making of political decisions. This is largely a result of the facts that government actions are often announced and carried out in a more open way than decisions are reached, and that generally many more persons are influenced by government activities than are involved in making government decisions.

2 Methods of political geographers

The methods used by political geographers are not different from those used by other geographers, but it seems worth while to include this chapter for two reasons. Firstly, political geographers have written very little about methods of research in their field; Wright (1944) is one of the few political geographers to have written specifically on this theme, although indications of useful methods will be found in textbooks by Pounds (1963) and de Blij (1967). Secondly, in the multitude of books published recently, which deal with research methods, particularly quantitative analysis, there is rarely any reference to political geography.

The point which is uniformly stressed by political geographers is the need for an objective viewpoint in research programmes. This is not meant to suggest that objectivity is more important in political geography than other branches of geography, but just that it is harder to achieve. It is difficult to think of anyone becoming emotionally involved about moraines, or port forelands, but many people would immediately take a mental position if the political geography of Israeli-occupied Arab lands or of Bantustan Homelands in South Africa was discussed. Objectivity cannot be taught as a subject such as map projections can be taught; indeed many would argue that perfect objectivity is impossible, and all political geographers must accept the chance that they have subconscious feelings which encourage them to select evidence in a partial fashion. There are a number of ways in which political geographers can try to maintain the highest level of objectivity possible, short of exploration of the subconscious through psychological examination. Firstly, the selection and interpretation of facts should be exposed to critical assessment by a number of different people with varying political viewpoints. Enthusiastic praise from one side and bitter condemnation from the other is not inconsistent with objectivity, but at least the criticisms raised can be taken into account in any re-valuation. Secondly, political geographers are advised to avoid deep political commitments for that is the road to the perversion of *Geopolitik*. This does not mean that political geographers should not enter political controversy. It simply means that they should not enter controversy as the adherent of one side or the other: their role should be that of an impartial specialist. For example, the views of an Australian political geographer about the geographical bases of Australian foreign policy and the views of an English political geographer on the British electoral redistribution must be treated with some reserve if they are committed members of one of the political parties involved. This leads naturally to the third suggestion. If a political geographer is unable to avoid a deep political commitment, he would be wise to confine his research to those areas unaffected by his bias. This warning applies especially to student political geographers; the first research topics should always be those where the students' political blinkers do not affect their vision.

There are three stages through which research in political geography should be conducted. Firstly, it is necessary to observe and collect the facts related to the subject. Secondly, the collected material must be organized and described. Finally, the organized material should be analysed so that the nature of the subject can be explained. The remainder of this chapter examines these three stages separately, although it is recognized that the stages are interlocking. For example, the organization of material in the second stage will generally be made with the requirements of the analytical techniques, to be used in the third stage, in mind; further, those analytical techniques will be tailored to suit the material which has been made available in the first stage.

Observation and collection of material

There are two parts to this original procedure. First a plan should be prepared to guide the collection of information and second that information must then be accumulated.

The plan devised to guide data collection will vary in complexity with the research theme. For example, if it is desired to investigate the evolution in position of a particular international boundary the plan could be quite simple. The following scheme is only one of several which could be used:

1. Identification of the number of countries involved and the period of negotiations.
2. Collection of information about exploration before and during negotiations, which would indicate the geographical knowledge available to diplomats at various times.
3. Examination of correspondence between governments and between members of a single government from the archives of all countries involved.
4. Accumulation of treaties concerning the boundary together with official maps throughout the negotiating period.

5. Perusal of the personal memoirs of individuals involved in the negotiations, and of citizens living in the borderland.
6. Survey of newspaper files during the period of negotiations.
7. Perusal of historical, geographical and biographical accounts which may include references to the boundary.
8. Fieldwork in the borderland.

In short this plan is designed to provide as much relevant material as possible. It would be much harder to produce a plan to study a less finite subject. For example, if it was decided to examine the political geography of secession, it would be necessary to define this term, to decide what measures of secession are most reliable and available, to select the examples to be considered, and to determine which of the many aspects of the political geography of secession will be studied. But whether the plan is straightforward or complicated it is essential in order to simplify the collection of information and to ensure that no important sources are overlooked.

In common with other human geographers political geographers have two prime sources of information: fieldwork and documents, using the latter term to include material in archives, maps, books, photographs, films, newspapers and recordings.

Fieldwork involves two principal activities: direct observation and interviews with people. Typical subjects suitable for direct observation include traffic counts across international boundaries; the significance of government policies for land-use patterns; and the state of a boundary's demarcation. Interviews with people will be usually of two kinds. First it will be useful to hold discussions with individuals who have been responsible for significant decisions. I have generally found it to be salutary to talk to members of parliament, party officials, local councillors, ambassadors, the leaders of pressure groups and public servants. Such people are concerned with practical politics and it is both refreshing and instructive to discuss topics of common interest with them. Discussions with officials involved in international relations will often reveal a very clear picture of the main recurring themes, and the significance attached by various governments to geographical facts. The real picture of diplomatic grand strategy is often much simpler than that painted by academic observers, who, looking in from the outside, have to find their clues through the content analyses of speeches and the interpretation of parliamentary debates. In their anxiety to avoid overlooking any relevant factor academics often introduce wholly unimportant factors into the analysis. It might be added that such officials invariably express their ideas in a simple language which some political geographers would do well to copy. Conversations with party officials are useful because they very often reveal a detailed appreciation of the political structure of electorates which a single fieldworker would take a lifetime to learn. Such party officials of course derive their information from long experience and the distillation of countless reports by campaign workers in many elections. Since people are usually conferring a favour by granting such an interview and are also concerned to put the best possible interpretation on their actions, it is well to be thoroughly prepared for the interview. A thorough knowledge of the indisputable facts and figures and carefully prepared questions will save time. It is also important to avoid antagonizing the person being interviewed, through the exposure of strong contrary opinions; these can always be expressed in the final text. Providing these rules are followed such individuals can be a rich source of information which is unavailable elsewhere. The second type of interview will be designed to find out the attitudes of a large number of people to a specific situation. Duverger (1964) distinguishes between *direct extensive observation*, where samples are used to analyse large communities, and *direct intensive observation*, where a small community or section is studied in depth. Political geographers will find both techniques useful and Duverger (1964), Young (1956) and Moser (1958) are representative of the many authors who have written clearly on the careful methods needed in framing questionnaires, selecting samples and conducting interviews, so that the information derived is not contaminated or biased. It would be useful, for example, to conduct extensive surveys to find out why people voted for a particular party along the lines of the study by Butler and Stokes (1969) into forces shaping electoral choice in Britain, and intensive surveys to discover the attitude of specific groups to the operation of government policies or to particular features of the political landscape.

While it is tempting to urge that there is no subject in political geography where fieldwork will not be useful it must be recognized that in some cases it is unlikely to be productive. Fieldwork will be most suitable in contemporary situations involving electoral attitudes and the operation of government policies, and in historical studies where past periods have left their imprint in the landscape. The location of castles in the Welsh Marches, and the relics of German political administration in Togoland, Southwest Africa, Kamerun and New Guinea, are subjects where fieldwork would be just as helpful as in the study of the landscape significance of the Canadian Government's policy to reduce wheat acreage in 1969–70, or in any analysis of the increased vote for the Democratic Labor Party in the Australian Senate elections of November 1970. Conversely, fieldwork is unlikely to be helpful in an analysis of historical events which have not left any imprint in the landscape, such as electoral trends in nineteenth-century Britain, or when the imprints require the specialized techniques of the archaeologist, such as a study of the Roman colonization of North Africa.

It is possible to classify documents in a variety of ways, but for political geographers it is useful to distinguish between primary and secondary sources. Primary sources are original documents, such as letters from one government to another, memoranda of government departments, personal diaries and air photographs; secondary sources result from the work of someone who has considered the primary sources and written about them; they include newspapers and books.

The richest store of primary sources is the various archives of national governments. Into such repositories are placed correspondence files, minutes of meetings and many other documents of interest to the political geographer. In many countries there are also local archives and these can be very important in federal states such as Australia. Regrettably not all government papers are lodged in archives, so it may be necessary to supplement these sources with others. Further, some archives were destroyed during the world wars of this century. But the political geographer is not only interested in the original documents of national and sub-national governments; the archives of trades unions and various pressure groups can be most enlightening in accounting for changes in government policies, or the variable areal success of some government policies, or past patterns of electoral support. It can often be difficult to obtain access to the records of pressure groups, such as a new state movement in Australia or India, and such records are often incomplete. It is probably easier for a member of such a group to obtain permission to peruse the available records, but it is correspondingly more difficult for such a person to maintain an impartial viewpoint in analysing the material. In most official archives there is a rule which prohibits the use of any material deposited within the last fifty years. This means that for this period the student must rely more heavily on other primary sources such as published international treaties, government gazettes with orders for boundary and regulation changes, parliamentary reports and published statistics. Very often the published statistics will be too general for detailed analysis and the scholar is then advised to seek access to the returns from which the final totals were computed. Certainly in Australia there is little excuse for students studying population to ignore the statistics for collectors' districts which are available from the appropriate departments. The difficulty of using old statistics is to find the boundaries of the areas to which they apply, and for this reason a collection of official maps showing electoral, municipal and statistical units is invaluable. Since the development of air photography a new valuable primary source has been added. These photographs are most useful in studying such subjects as the development of borderlands and the significance of government policies to land development.

With all primary sources there are two problems associated with the extraction of information. It is first necessary to establish the validity of the document, and second it is essential to assess its accuracy. The validity of most documents in archives is not in dispute, although ancient documents may sometimes create controversy. If there is any doubt, then the geographer is advised to seek the assistance of an expert in documents. The chance of forgery is greater where a country finds that there is insufficient or contradictory evidence in its archives for a particular position it is taking in international negotiations. Rumours have been circulating in academic circles that more than one Asian power has been tampering with maps and reports in archives, to create favourable arguments in respect of territorial disputes. An assessment of the accuracy of any document must rest on the access which the author had to the facts of the situation, and his interest in reporting them honestly. There is reason to be more suspicious of memoranda written after some event with the benefit of hindsight, than reports written while the situation was developing.

In using government reports it is always necessary to guard against propaganda. Blatant propaganda, such as that published by the New China News Agency is easy to identify; it is more difficult to identify the bias contained in reports which are apparently factual and moderately written. Skill in distinguishing the worthwhile from the spurious in government publications can only be acquired with experience and continual cross-checking and questioning. Political geographers with a particular regional interest should certainly cultivate contacts with the diplomatic representatives of the countries making up the region; such sources provide much factual material about government policies, administrative changes and economic developments which cannot always be easily obtained elsewhere. It follows of course that such sources will be more productive if the political geographer is known to be an objective scholar.

Duverger (1964) distinguishes between the *classical* and *quantitative* analyses of primary sources. The classical methods are intensive and generally related to comparatively few documents. He stresses that it is important to study both the content of the document, which he calls internal analysis and the context and influence of the document which he calls external analysis. Clearly it is vital to know the audience at which the document was aimed to judge its influence. The extraction of facts, such as dates and quantities from primary sources leaves no room for disagreement among scholars, but problems arise when it is necessary to interpret the weight given to different qualitative arguments. Certainly no opportunity should be lost to compare information about a single situation from a variety of sources as a check against gross error in a single source.

I have not seen any example of the quantitative analysis of primary sources by a political geographer, but there is an interesting example of the technique applied to ice formation in some lakes on the Canadian Prairies by Catchpole, Moodie and Kaye (1970). It is possible to establish an accurate picture of the style of a particular writer by counting classes of words in the text, identifying the concordance between words and isolating the basic vocabulary. This is very useful in testing the validity of authorship, and it has also been used to complete gaps in the original text of the Dead Sea Scrolls. This does not seem a useful method for political geographers. When the scholar deals with ideas and themes in the document instead of words, the method called content analysis seems more appropriate. Berelson (1952) has noted that content analysis succeeds or fails by its categories, and in his book, and the books by Lasswell andLeites (1949) and Schutz (1950) there is a thorough discussion of the problems of identifying categories. These problems are probably greater for political scientists and historians than political geographers because of the slighter interest which the latter has in personalities and abstract political concepts. For most political geographers it is likely that a simple set of topical categories would suffice.

The two main secondary sources are newspapers and books, although it is quite possible that in the future sound recordings and films will also be included in this category. Newspapers have two main values to political geographers. Firstly, they help to provide the chronology of negotiations and developments in which political geographers may be interested, whether the subject is a secessionist movement, a colonial war or a programme of building strategic railways. Secondly, they give an excellent impression of the general context of the particular development. They give an indication of possibly related contemporary events, and the general attitudes of the populace to various proposed policies. Newspapers are notorious for having a biased viewpoint and it is useful to compare accounts about the same event from newspapers with a known range of views. In recent years there are some publications which gather news for particular regions from all the most important newspapers concerned. The *Africa Research Bulletin* and the *Arab World* are the best examples of such regional research aids; *Keesings Archives* and *Facts on File* provide a useful world coverage. Mrs X. Kasperson (Kasperson and Minghi 1969) has provided a useful, though not exhaustive, list of bibliographical research aids which political geographers should find helpful. Gleaning facts from books requires that the scholar should cast his net as wide as possible and cross-check all the facts recorded thoroughly.

The blend of factual sources used will depend on the time period being studied, and the subject and region under consideration. Archival material will be more complete for a longer period in states located in Europe than they will be for most of the newly independent countries of Asia and Africa, and relic features in borderlands will survive longer in temperate than in tropical areas. Some historical subjects, such as electoral patterns, do not lend themselves to fieldwork. Looking at the time period under consideration it is clear that contemporary studies will have to be conducted without access to archives. The main sources in such situations will be fieldwork, official reports and material prepared by pressure groups and press reports. As the analysis extends into the past fifty years an increasing range of secondary sources will become available, and in many cases fieldwork will still be appropriate. In periods more than fifty years ago, archival material will be accessible and the volume of secondary sources will swell, but the opportunities for fieldwork will be correspondingly limited because many of the decision-makers of that period will have died, and much of the landscape evidence which is significant will have been destroyed. Research into remote historical periods may have to be based entirely on secondary sources if original documents have been lost, or if there were no documents of any kind. An attempt to reconstruct the distribution of tribes and frontiers in the lower Niger about 1860 had to be based mainly on secondary sources by travellers, historians and anthropologists supplemented by rare letters in British archives (Prescott 1967).

The description of collected evidence

Ideally the process of description paves the way for analysis and explanation, but there are reasons, in certain circumstances, why description may be an end in itself. Firstly, some geographers are better at description than explanation and it would be a waste of their obvious talents to deny them outlets. Secondly, in some cases explanation will have to await the opening of archives or private papers in the distant future, yet the new development should be described by a contemporary scholar if possible. Such accounts generally have a greater value for future scholars than reconstructions attempted many years later. Thirdly, in some cases the explanation of a single situation or development may be made easier by comparison with a number of similar situations or developments. Since geographers can never have first-hand experience of all the cases which might be relevant it is very helpful to find such cases described by another. It is for the last two reasons that sections such as 'The changing world' in *Geography*, the 'Geographical Record' in the *Geographical Review* and *Cartactual* are such useful publications.

The techniques of description are well known though not always well applied in modern literature. Over the years geographers have developed precise shorthand methods of recording information on maps, on photographs and in diagrams. Books by Monkhouse and Wilkinson (1971) and Raisz (1948) outline such methods very carefully and make expansion of this aspect here unnecessary. Political geographers should not hesitate to use the full range of descriptive aids where appropriate; they should also criticize the careless use of these aids, especially maps, by historians, political scientists and journalists. But description also requires the presentation of statistics and written texts, and the basis of good description in this form is classification.

Harvey (1969, ch. 18) has provided a very precise account of classification in geography, which he describes as 'a filter through which we transform sense-perception data for a given purpose'. Failure to understand this fact has led too many political geographers to spend too much time trying to develop elaborate classifications of nation-states, of boundaries and of government policies which will serve all purposes and stand for all time. Unfortunately subjects such as these are so complex and have so many facets that no single scheme will satisfy all needs. Individual scholars must develop their own classifications for the particular aspect they are studying, and recognize that if the emphasis of research changes the old classification might have to be modified.

In developing any classification there are some simple criteria against which its usefulness can be tested. Firstly, is the classification comprehensive? The classification should cater for all the known cases to be effective. Secondly, are the various classes mutually exclusive, or are there instances where some case may fit equally well into two classes? If the classes are not mutually exclusive it may be necessary to resort to quantitative methods to assign all the cases objectively. Thirdly, is the classification such that different scholars would assign all selected cases to identical groups? If there are questions of interpretation it will reduce the value of the classification as a comparative tool. In political geography the most valuable classifications, such as Harts-horne's classes of boundaries according to their relation to settlement, are comprehensive, mutually exclusive, and easy to interpret.

Analysis and explanation

The aim of any analysis in political geography should be total explanation, although it must be recognized that in certain situations this will be impossible and the student will have to settle for a partial explanation. There are many different paths of analysis leading to explanation, and the path selected will depend upon the nature of the information collected and the abilities of the scholar. There is no reason why different methods of analysis should not be used to cross-check results, nor why different methods should not be employed to extract the maximum amount of insight from different aspects of a single research topic. Four types of analysis will be considered in this section; they are cartographic, classical, comparative and mathematical.

Only the techniques of cartographic analysis have been developed by geographers and then borrowed by workers in other disciplines. The other three techniques are not peculiar to any discipline and contributions to their refinement have come from many fields. Cartographic analysis involves studying the areal distribution of a single element of the political landscape, such as constituency boundaries, or examining the areal coincidence of a number of possibly related elements, such as areas of party preponderance and the ethnic structure of the electorate. The technique is most fruitfully employed at the largest possible scales, which enable the student to focus on fine details. It is also helpful in studying related elements which are statistically recorded in different territorial units. The matching of statistics is a serious problem and the comparison of carefully drawn maps using different territorial units, such as electorates and censal districts, can often be just as illuminating as the manipulation of data according to a series of debatable premises. The examination of a variety of distribution maps is also helpful in identifying regions which are of course a prime type of geographical classification.

The most distinguished example of cartographic analysis in political geography in recent years is the study of the impact of Negro migration on the electoral geography of Flint, Michigan by Lewis (1965). This method simply involves the plotting of some ethnic characteristic by choropleth shading and voting behaviour by isopleths on a single map (see fig. 2.1). Lewis offers this method as an alternative to the tedious and costly manipulation of censal and electoral statistics from different units, the collecting of sample surveys, and the use of sample precincts which fall entirely within one census tract. He recognizes that the method has limitations where small minorities of the group being investigated are swamped in a particular area by persons with different characteristics, and where large electoral units, created because of the low population density, include people of very diverse qualities. The method is most useful where the group under consideration occupies a discrete area and where the voting is very partisan. This technique also has the cardinal virtue of being appropriate to historical studies where sample surveys are impossible. Lewis also suggests that such maps may be very useful in revealing voting inconsistencies which may merit closer field investigation. He cites the case of certain Democratic bastions which stand out in the Republican stronghold of rural, central Pennsylvania for no immediately apparent reason. Political geographers have not been quick to follow Lewis' lead and it is to be regretted that other interests in historical geography have prevented him from pursuing the lines he suggested.

One of the most interesting attempts to use cartographic analysis to identify a political region was made by Woolmington (1966), who studied the support for the separatist movement in northern New South Wales. This method involves the superimposition of five maps, each of which showed the distribution of a single political criterion

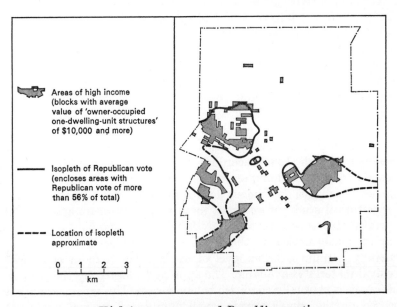

Areas of high income
(blocks with average
value of 'owner-occupied
one-dwelling-unit structures'
of $10,000 and more)

Isopleth of Republican vote
(encloses areas with
Republican vote of more
than 56% of total)

Location of isopleth
approximate

0   1   2   3
      km

2.1 *High income areas and Republican voting,
Flint, Michigan, 1950.*

which showed support for the new state movement. This made it possible to distinguish the core region where all the criteria were present from peripheral areas where only some of the criteria existed. There are two main requirements for this method to be successful; the first is accuracy in drawing and the second is the ability to compare the criteria in terms of significance. It is obviously important to avoid using two criteria which measure the same features. To take an extreme example, it would not help to show strong support for the Labour Party *and* weak support for the Conservative Party to identify political regions in England; it would be sufficient to show one or the other. There will be cases where the identity of two criteria will not be so obvious, and thorough cross-checking is always necessary. Any use of this method should always include an assessment of the reliability of the criteria so that the reader can make his own interpretation of the results.

Cartographic analysis is also useful in identifying the extent to which boundaries delimiting various political areas coincide, either at a particular point in time, or over some period of history. Such maps give an insight into features in the landscape, such as rivers or main roads, which have been regarded as clear dividing lines by boundary-makers. In some cases the persistence of boundaries in an apparently uniform area will suggest the previous existence of some former cultural division or landscape feature which has now disappeared. The map of boundary permanence in India and Pakistan prepared by Spate (1957, 147) is a striking example of the value of this method.

Cartographic analysis may clearly be an integral part of the other forms of analysis to be discussed, and in many cases the material to be mapped will first need to be statistically transformed.

Classical analysis here refers to the painstaking and thorough reconstruction of all relevant aspects of a single event or a series of closely related events. All sources will be used but there will be heaviest reliance on fieldwork and primary documents. The study by Nicholson (1954) dealing with the evolution of Canada's boundaries and the account by Lamb (1966) recording the evolution of the McMahon line between India and China, are excellent examples of classical analysis. The heavy reliance on primary documents often means that the subject is a historical study of an event more than fifty years ago; it is also generally true that classical analysis will rarely employ any but the simplest mathematical methods. Where the subject is more recent it generally permits a lower level of explanation than in cases where archival material is available. The approach adopted by the scholar in this analysis is usually cognitive behaviourism. This means attention is focused on the comparatively small number of persons significantly involved in the situation, such as cabinet ministers, rulers and delegates to international conferences. Any particular classical analysis will not produce laws because it is concerned with a single specific event which occurs in a unique area at a unique time. At the same time there is plenty of evidence to show that continuing classical analysis in a particular area will enable the student concerned to predict the outcome of particular developments with some confidence. For example, in November, 1965, I contributed to a radio discussion in Melbourne on the future of Rhodesia, and took the position that Rhodesia should be able to survive for the foreseeable future. This was not an original view since many other objective commentators around the world had reached similar conclusions; it is the reasons why this view seemed sensible which are interesting. *At that time* it seemed certain that there was considerable potential for economic diversification in Rhodesia; that South Africa and Portugal would not co-operate fully with United Nations calls for sanctions; that individual businessmen around the world would see lucrative opportunities in breaching the wall of sanctions and that Britain would have to operate sanctions carefully to avoid damaging the Zambian economy until it had time to make the necessary adjustments. Prediction in other situations, such as Vietnam, is fraught with great uncertainty because of the many variables involved. However, where political geographers have made detailed studies of areas, and where simple situations seem to develop, it is often worth while to make predictions and test them against the eventual outcome. This can be most helpful in sharpening critical faculties and revealing factors which had been previously overlooked.

While a single classical analysis cannot produce useful generalizations or laws, it is possible to gain real insight by comparing two or more analyses of different subjects. This is the basis of the comparative method. Obviously the two cases being compared must be neither identical nor completely different; it is essential that there should be both common and distinctive elements. There are three general types of comparison for the political geographer. Firstly, it is possible to compare two distinct areas at the same period of time. For example, it would be illuminating to compare the secessionist movements in Nigeria, Uganda and the Sudan in the period from 1967 to 1970, or the government policies adopted in respect of wheat production in Canada, Australia and the United States in the period 1968–70. Such investigations would show the operation of different geographical factors in a uniform international context. Secondly, it is interesting to compare events which occur in a single area at different times. Such examinations will reveal how changes in technical skills and the international environment will vary the significance of individual geographical factors. The study by Helin (1967) of Roumania's internal boundaries provides a very good example of this kind of comparative study. Thirdly, it is possible to compare different areas at different times, although it would be necessary for some procedural link to be present. For example, it would be useful to compare the political geography of the process of decolonization in South America and Africa, or the process of territorial expansion by Rome and Spain, or the dissolution of the Turkish and Austro-Hungarian Empires. The analyses of Fisher (1962 and 1968) dealing with a comparison of the Balkans and South-East Asia and Britain and Japan respectively are good examples of the usefulness of this technique.

Spykman (1933) proposed an examination of the significance of domestic and external factors for the formation of foreign policy, by comparing situations when one of these groups of factors seemed to be constant. There is no evidence that Spykman or anyone else used the concept successfully, and it is hard to think of cases where this method would be appropriate.

While geographers have long used simple mathematical techniques to analyse statistics, in recent years more advanced mathematical procedures have become fashionable. Several books dealing with these techniques have appeared (Gregory 1963; Cole and King 1968) and some journals are devoted to articles using and discussing mathematical analysis. This development has made it necessary for geographers to learn new words which have very precise meanings. Coincident with this increase in the use of mathematical analysis has been the growth in the use of models, which have the common characteristic of being simplified representations of actual situations or processes. The trend towards mathematical analysis and models has not been as marked in political geography as in some other aspects of the subject. Few of the experts in mathematical techniques refer to political geography in their general texts; only Cole and King (1968, 621–30) attempt to provide a detailed coverage.

The strongest statement about the need for mathematical analysis was made by Berry when he wrote an enthusiastic review of the study of international regions by Russett (1967).

> ... Russett's analysis is fundamentally and consistently geographical, even though he is a political scientist and subtitles his work 'A study in political ecology'. What might political geography, that moribund backwater, become with an infusion of work of this kind? (Berry 1969)

The short answer to this question must be that the moribund backwater would become a dangerous swamp. Political geographers trapped there would be uncertain of their footing and orientation and would soon exhaust their energy. My careful reading of Russett's book leads me to agree with Young, a political scientist who wrote a long and detailed review of the work.

> ... it (is) difficult to avoid being impressed by the essential futility of the exercise ...

> Russett has become so pre-occupied with the intricacies of various techniques for the manipulation of data that he has seriously neglected a number of critical and antecedent problems of epistemology and theory. The result is an elaborate presentation of data whose purposes are unclear and whose utility is undermined by the absence of an adequate conceptual foundation. (Young 1969, 486)

Most of Berry's shotgun criticism of political geography misses the mark, and suggests an unfamiliarity with the target. However, he is correct in suggesting that political geographers should experiment with mathematical techniques which have proved useful in other branches of geography. Before such a trend is hailed as the salvation of political geography it is necessary to explore the extent of opportunities for mathematical analysis.

In an effort to discover the extent to which models and mathematical techniques were used in political geography, letters were sent to some thirty writers of political geography and sixteen replies were received. Only three of the respondents had never used models of any kind; by contrast nine of the scholars consulted had not used any statistical techniques, apart from the calculation of percentages and means. It was noticeable that those who had used other mathematical techniques were generally younger men. To discover more precisely the scope which existed in political geography for the use of mathematical techniques three lists were prepared. The first (fig. 2.2) contains those aspects of the political geography of states which could be measured by one of the four systems of measurement – nominal, ordinal, interval and ratio. The second list (fig. 2.3) represents those aspects of political geography which have been subject to mathematical analysis, and the third list (fig. 2.4) comprises those aspects of political geography which are clearly unsuited to measurement and mathematical analysis.

It is not proposed to discuss fig. 2.2 in detail. Other political geographers might wish to add certain aspects of human behaviour, such as attitudes to a new government regulation, which can be measured for a sample population. Providing such measurements are carried out in accordance with the precise methods established by psychologists and others there can be no objection to their use. It is apparent that there are many subjects which can be precisely measured and it is interesting to concentrate on those aspects of political geography which have been subject to mathematical analysis.

Although boundaries can be measured accurately in terms of length, duration and direction little use has been made of these measurements. Boggs (1940) produced some ratios which compared the political fragmentation of continents, related the shape of the country to its boundary, and purported to indicate the population pressure against any particular boundary. While the first two are useful, Hinks (1940) showed the serious fallacy in the third, and apart from its use by Hamdan (1963) it has been ignored. Ratios to measure the sinuosity of boundaries, devised by Dorion (1963), seem to have very limited usefulness.

Movements of messages, people, goods and capital across boundaries can also be measured and there have been attempts to use them for two distinct purposes. Mackay (1958) suggested that the significance of the boundary as an obstacle in the landscape could be measured by an application of the interactance hypothesis. His interesting paper has not been followed by the widespread testing that might have been

Fig. 2.2

A list of selected features of the political landscape and other political items of interest to political geographers which can be accurately measured.

BOUNDARIES

Length
Number of official crossing points
Some aspects of traffic across the boundary
The means by which sections of the boundary are demarcated
Duration
Width of territorial waters, neutral zones and other areal
  features

NATIONAL CAPITAL

Population
Employment structure
Absolute and relative location
Duration
Government expenditure on buildings

INTERNAL ADMINISTRATIVE DIVISIONS

Number of classes of divisions, and numbers within each class
Length of internal boundaries
Area
Population
Budget of each unit
Some aspects of economic output
Volume of selected contacts between units

ELECTIONS

Number of candidates
Number of votes for each candidate
Number of votes for each party
Number of electorates
Size of electorates in terms of voters and area
Number of polling booths
Votes in assemblies

ECONOMIC PRODUCTION OF POLITICAL UNITS

Output of various industries
Employment structure and distribution
Some internal movement of goods, capital and people

POPULATION

Structure in respect of various characteristics
Numbers
Distribution

Fig. 2.2—Continued

PERSONAL POLITICAL BEHAVIOUR

Sample surveys of voting attitudes, attitudes to government policies and political features, such as boundaries and capitals.

INTERNATIONAL ECONOMIC CONTACTS

Trade
Announced aid programmes
Membership of international economic organisations
Migration
Capital flow
Total of ships, planes, trains and vehicles involved

INTERNATIONAL POLITICAL AND STRATEGIC CONTACTS

War in terms of duration and casualties
Diplomats exchanged
Membership of strategic and political
*   organizations*
Location of troops and bases
Visits by heads of state
Movement of refugees

expected. The apparent neglect may result from two characteristics of such investigations.

Firstly, it may be very difficult to isolate the significance of the boundary from the significance of some physical feature, such as a major river or mountain range with which the boundary coincides. Secondly, it may be very difficult to obtain an accurate count of important interactions relating to the movement of people, capital and goods across a particular *segment* of boundary. Telephone calls have been used but many political geographers would be reluctant to place too much weight on such evidence. The second use of statistics relating to boundary traffic is to make inferences about the relations between the countries concerned. Soja (1968) examined the changes in the volume of telephone calls among Kenya, Uganda and Tanzania and related them to changes in enthusiasm among the leaders of these countries for the proposed East African Federation. The results were interesting but it is certain that a clearer picture would have been provided by the detailed analysis of speeches by the leaders, trade among the countries and internal political development. At the best his evidence provided additional support for trends already well known to any student of African political geography.

Reynolds and McNulty (1968) have made a plea for political geographers to study the influence of political boundaries on the behaviour

Fig. 2.3

A list of selected topics in political geography which have been analysed by mathematical techniques.

BOUNDARIES

Interaction across the boundary
Shape of territory enclosed
Alignment of boundary
Attitudes towards the boundary by individuals

STATE POLICIES

The relations between the decision-maker's background and his attitude to policy formation
The relations between particular situations and particular policies
The relations between intended and actual policy results

NATIONAL INTEGRATION

Links between various parts of a single state and between states considering federation

ELECTIONS

Classifying voting groups at the United Nations
Identifying crucial issues at the United Nations
Explaining voting patterns

NATIONAL POWER

Ranking of states according to calculated power

INTERNATIONAL POLITICAL REGIONS

Classification of states by political criteria

Fig. 2.4

A list of selected topics in political geography which seem unsuitable for mathematical analysis.

The evolution of boundaries and frontiers and territorial disputes
The formation of international alliances
The political geography of any country where statistics are inadequate
The political geography of any past period when statistics are inadequate
Most aspects of territorial disintegration, such as secession, decolonization and conquest
Most aspects of territorial evolution
The evolution of a national capital
Much specific policy-making

of individuals. They argue that citizens perceive boundaries in different terms and will shape their behaviour to match their impressions, whether the subject under examination is movement for work or shopping, or long-term migration. The precise information on which this investigation depends must be collected through interviews with individuals selected randomly, or because of their membership of groups with uniform characteristics. Reynolds and McNulty are in no doubt about the value of such studies:

> Therefore, analysis aimed at specifying the disruptive effects of boundaries more precisely (and particularly quantitatively) would be of considerable import for the development of both theory and policy. (p. 34)

Such studies have yet to be made on a scale which will demonstrate their true worth, but if they are possible and successful they will supplement the more traditional investigation by political geographers of the attitudes of governments to boundaries. Clearly the attitudes of the government must be established first, because as a result of these attitudes, regulations will be framed which influence the perception of the boundary developed by individuals.

Another aspect of political geography which has been subject to mathematical analysis is the power of the state. There have been many attempts to derive a formula for measuring state power which allow comparisons to be made between states at the same time, or between the situation of a single state at two different times. None of these attempts has enjoyed any success whatsoever. Fortunately in recent years geographers appear to have wasted less time in this exercise than scholars in other disciplines. For example, German (1960) produced an elaborate calculation which lists area, corrected for population and rail densities; population, corrected for technical efficiency and morale; industrial production of steel, coal, lignite, petroleum and hydro-electricity; military personnel, uncorrected for skill or equipment or morale; and an index of nuclear strength. The square kilometres, people, tons of coal, soldiers and nuclear index are then added together to give a grand total which represents the state's power ranking. This elaborate exercise clearly illustrates the futility of the search for a single index of state power which will allow states to be compared. Apart from the fact that there would be little agreement among analysts on the corrections applied to any single state in respect of morale or technical efficiency, the formula takes no account of the quality of leadership, ignores location and assumes that the possession of un-occupied or lightly occupied territory is an unmitigated disadvantage.

A more dogmatic formula for power has been advanced by Fucks (1965) who is a professional physicist. He calculated the power index from the combination of figures relating to population, steel production and fuel production in Bernouilli differential equations and other mathematical devices. By trial and error methods he juggled the three sets of figures until he reached a combination which best reflected the power ratings of the states concerned in 1960. The formula is:

$$M = P^3\sqrt{B}$$

where M represents power (*Macht*), P represents production and B represents population (*Bevolkerungszahl*). By application of this formula, after the construction of graphs to show predicted increases in numbers of people and economic output, Fucks was able to assert that by 1970 China's power should surpass that of the Soviet Union, and that by 1975 China will be the most powerful state in the world! Michaels (1966) reviewing this book noted that by restricting himself to measurable factors, Fucks' formula avoided the 'vague concepts, suppositions and speculations that have often marred traditional geo-political studies' (p. 305). It must be realized that the fact that some factors cannot be measured does not mean that they can be ignored. But perhaps the real criticism of these power analyses is that they never discuss the purpose to which the power is applied. The power of the Soviet Union to take successful action in Czechoslovakia differs from its power to take successful action in the Middle East or Cuba.

Aspects of government policy have also been analysed by mathe-matical techniques, although geographers have done less in this field than political scientists. Sewell (1968) investigated the attitude of engineers to water resources and their management in British Columbia, and the ways in which particular attitudes appear to have influenced public policy. The analysis was based on the responses of thirty en-gineers to a questionnaire; it confirmed that people view water as an important contributor to the maintenance of the economy; that municipal waste-disposal managers regard streams and aquifers as suitable for waste disposal unless it can be shown that there is direct damage to others; that managers regard floods as fluctuations which there is a public duty to control, and that economic considerations are ignored in evaluations involving the competition between fisheries and other uses, because the value of preserving nature is regarded as para-mount (Sewell 1968, 42–3). The study was unable to assess the sig-nificance of the engineers' attitudes because no investigation was made of the attitudes of other groups, such as politicians and economists, who are also involved in decision-making. The results of Sewell's survey do not contain any surprises, but they do show that it is worth while to seek information through fieldwork involving sample surveys.

It should be possible to use mathematical techniques theoretically to investigate the relationships between a particular situation and government policies used to deal with such situations. For example, government policies towards domestic manufacturing industries could be related to the nature of international trade patterns. A political scientist has tried to investigate the conditions associated with war as a government policy. Wallace (1969) examined the relationships between national status-inconsistency and international war. National status-inconsistency is the discrepancy between the status which a country *achieves* through its economic and military capacity, and the status which it is *ascribed* by other states in the international system. Achieved status was measured by five indicators: population, urban population, iron and steel production, armed forces and military expenditure. Ascribed status was measured by the number of diplomatic missions received by any state. The level of status inconsistency for the whole international system was then calculated by adding the rank order differences of the five achieved status indicators and the ascribed status indicator. These five international totals for five year periods were then correlated with the level of international war measured by number of casualties and the duration of fighting. This correlation satisfied Wallace that national status inconsistency was strongly associated with the magnitude and severity of war ten to fifteen years later, even though a regression equation showed that the five variables considered accounted for only 38% of the variance in the levels of war. For some reason, which is difficult to understand, Wallace was unable to demonstrate that any of the states which experienced status inconsistency were also the states involved in some way with the resulting wars. It is to be hoped that geographers will profit from Wallace's bad example and avoid grandiose investigations based on such debatable measurements. Roos (1969) has shown that there is much more profit in making mathematical analyses of detailed situations. He investigated the characteristics of sixty-seven Turkish provincial governors and correlated his findings with the attitudes of the governors to economic development. He specifically examined the extent to which the governors were in favour of the fastest possible economic development for their area, regardless of inequalities, or whether they preferred a rate of development which spread the advantages uniformly throughout the province.

Electoral statistics are among the most precise which are available to political geographers. It is therefore not surprising that this field has seen a greater use of mathematical techniques than any other aspect of the subject. Generally electoral geographers, and others interested in this field, have had one of two aims in using these mathematical techniques. Some have sought to explain the pattern of voting in particular areas at specific times. Others have tried to identify voting groups in international assemblies. There are many studies representative of the first kind of analysis, and these will be considered in greater detail in the chapter dealing with electoral geography. The example briefly considered here, was provided by McPhail (1970), who examined the characteristics of voting in the Los Angeles mayoral election of 1969. After adjusting the votes cast to censal districts McPhail made a factor analysis involving forty-one variables. These were collapsed to eight factor patterns of which four were judged to be relevant. McPhail shows a greater realism in carrying out his investigation than some electoral geographers; he does not ignore the significance of the campaign's issues or the personalities of candidates standing for election. There are many questions at the end which must be left unanswered; for example, it is impossible to know whether the Negro candidate was rejected primarily because of a conservative reaction on the law-and-order issue, or a reaction by White voters to his racial qualities; further, there is no explanation of why voters whose original first choices were eliminated in the primary election switched mainly to Mayor Yorty in the decisive election. But this investigation identified the key areas within which detailed local analyses should be made by someone wanting to probe more deeply.

Factor analysis has also been used to distinguish crucial issues at the United Nations and groups of states who persistently seem to vote the same way. The best-known studies are by Alker (1964 and 1965), Russett (1966) and Friedheim (1967). Friedheim's study was concerned with the United Nations conferences on the law of the sea held in 1958 and 1960. At the two conferences, representatives were asked to vote on seventy-eight issues. By using these seventy-eight votes as variables in an R-analysis seven significant issues were identified and Friedheim then went on to study how the various participants grouped themselves on these issues. He recommended this analysis to international lawyers who would see more clearly why this conference failed in certain areas, and when a problem may be virtually insoluble. It would be useful for political geographers to carry out such investigations in order to identify those issues which have a significant geographical component, and to discover which countries have a common attitude to such issues. For example, two of the important issues noted by Friedheim of interest to geographers concerned the rights of coastal states to control fishing in their own adjacent waters, and the right of landlocked countries to have access to the sea.

Before attempting such a study the political geographer should be aware of some of the assumptions which have to be made, and which may not always apply. Friedheim frankly notes some of these difficulties.

There is no implicit ordinal 'significance' scale isomorphic to a nation's assigned voting rank when the rank is based only on the relationship between that vote and all others cast on the same ballot. In addition, there are a number of motives other than 'significance of the issue' that may cause a nation to take an extreme stand. (Friedheim 1967, 56)

Young (1969) has also questioned some of the assumptions made by Russett in using factor analysis to establish the relative significance of internal and external factors in shaping a state's foreign policy. Russett (1966) suggested that since voting patterns in the United Nations remained nearly constant from 1952 to 1963, against a background of domestic political changes, the explanation must be sought in the operation of factors in the international system. The first assumption is that votes in the General Assembly are an accurate reflection of the state's performance in world politics, whereas many votes really reflect the knowledge of the representatives that whatever the outcome of the voting there will be no subsequent actions by the United Nations. The second assumption is that continuity in voting patterns is due to the unchanging quality of a small number of factors, while they may be due to offsetting changes in a larger number of factors. However, providing the political geographer ensures that his analysis requires only a few, sensible assumptions insight may be gained by factor analysis of votes in international assemblies. The United Nations is certainly best suited because of the larger number of states involved, and the multiplicity of votes taken.

Carter (1969) made one of the few attempts to apply mathematical methods to the study of historical political geography, when he analysed the medieval Serbian oecumene during the reign of Stefan Dusan (1331–55). Carter used connectivity analysis, eigen values and the measurement of accessibility to identify the oecumene of the Serbian state and to decide whether Stefan Dusan had made the right choice in Skoplje as his capital. These methods deal with the number of direct connections each centre has with other centres, the number of eleven step routes which can be used in going out from and back to each settlement, and the total mileage needed to travel from one centre to all the other centres. These calculations lead Carter to conclude that 'the Serbian oecumene seems to have extended further west than has hitherto been realized' and that Stefan Dusan's capital 'does not theoretically appear to have been the best'. Carter also speculates that had a more central capital been adopted, the disorders and rebellions, which enabled the more remote parts of the Empire to assert their independence on the death of Stefan Dusan, might have been avoided. Carter makes only two basic assumptions; first, that the degree of connectivity of the centres is directly related to the human activity in these places, and second, that with a uniform means of transport by donkey, time taken would vary directly with distance. It is doubtful if these assumptions are sufficient. Traffic between areas is more probably related to the population and economic activities of the centres, and there is no guarantee that in the fourteenth century all the routes considered were equally safe. In view of the very tentative conclusions reached after several pages of calculation and manipulation, it would seem that further applications will be necessary to establish the usefulness of this type of analysis.

Fig. 2.4 lists some of the more important aspects of political geography which do not seem to be suitable for mathematical analysis. The list is self-explanatory and it is only necessary to comment that many of the aspects relate to subjects of prime concern to political geographers – the development and disintegration of states and empires. The evolution of states, the acquisition of colonies, the formation of boundaries, boundary disputes and the breakdown of empires are subjects which have been well developed by political geographers, yet in no case has mathematical analysis of the more advanced kind improved our understanding of processes or causes. This statement is made in the light of the interesting studies in integration made by Soja (1968) and Witthuhn (1968) and the study of medieval Serbia by Carter (1969). It also seems likely that important sections of the increasingly popular study of geography and policy will also rely mainly on qualitative rather than quantitative methods.

There are a number of problems which make mathematical analysis difficult or inappropriate; some are common to all branches of geography, some are peculiar to political geography. Firstly, at the nation state level, which is the level at which so much political geography is conducted, there is a shortage of cases. The number of independent states is less than 140; they operate under such a variety of systems that the number contained in any group, which is homogeneous in respect of only one or two characteristics is likely to be less than twenty. If the number of characteristics is increased the total in any single group will be correspondingly reduced. This difficulty is more acute in political geography where there is a greater diversity of political characteristics to study, than in economic and urban geography where there are fewer crucial differences between states. Secondly, it is easier to measure contacts between states in respect of economic activities than in respect of political acts. Economic and population geographers can obtain fairly accurate nominal measurements of the volume of trade and the number of migrants linking the United States and Western Europe. The political geographer would have to measure political links between these two areas by such unreliable items as the number of American troops in Europe, the location of American bases in Europe, the common membership of international organizations, the exchange of diplomatic representatives, visits by the heads of state and the content analysis of speeches and reports. Any one of these measurements is unsatisfactory by itself, but there are large problems in deciding the differing degrees of reliance which should be placed on each. Thirdly, there is the problem common to all branches of geography that in many parts of the world reliable statistics are not available. Unfortunately this lack occurs mainly in the underdeveloped countries of Africa, Asia and South America where some of the clearest connections between geography and politics are evident. Geographers such as Spate, Buchanan, Kibulya, Langlands, de Blij and McGee who have made useful studies in these areas have done so without the benefit of advanced mathematical methods. Fourthly, just as comparisons at the nation state level are difficult, so are comparisons of the internal political geographies of individual states. It is particularly unfortunate that electoral geography, where mathematical methods have been most fruitful, is particularly difficult to study mathematically on a comparative basis. Comparative studies can be made of rural weighting and gerrymandering, but the diversity of parties makes behavioural comparisons very difficult.

Sometimes it may be possible to make comparative mathematical analyses of the internal administrative structure of states, but it is hard to imagine how such a study would be constructed and what its intrinsic value would be. Fortunately, if one is concerned with the internal political geography of a single state some of the difficulties disappear. Mathematical analysis of the equivalent units throughout a country, such as Australian federal states, Canadian provinces, British rural districts or French communes seems both possible and useful whether the study is concerned with individual characteristics or the level of interactance between units. The fifth difficulty relates to the lack of ready-made theories which political geographers can import from political science. There is no equivalent to Weber, Lösch or Hoover in political science to provide theories which can be tested by field measurements. Such theory as is produced by political scientists is of a qualitative nature which it is very difficult to test mathematically without losing much contact with reality. The sixth difficulty, which is peculiar to political geography concerns the variations available in political motive. While economic geographers recently have claimed to identify motives other than profit there has always seemed to be a larger number of political motives. Some politicians seem to have a greater commitment to international accord than to national advantage; some fashion policies to attract support while others, admittedly a few, put principles before power; some desire power to promote change, some to preserve the presents ituation. Further, while there are a number of fairly simple measurements of economic success there would be little general agreement as to the best measure of political success. The final problem is common to all branches of geography; it concerns the difficulties which geographers using mathematical methods face in communicating with geographers unversed in these techniques. There is a real danger that unless attention is paid to this problem the estrangement between quantitative and qualitative geographers will become complete. A whole new vocabulary has emerged with the use of advanced mathematical techniques; many traditional geographers have not bothered to learn about it, many modern geographers speak no other language. As a result of this situation there is very little intellectual contact between the two groups.

In addition to identifying the problems it is important to suggest possible solutions, and it may be helpful to suggest courses of action to both traditional political geographers and those who use advanced mathematical techniques. The first thing for traditional geographers to realize is that there is no need for competition with mathematical analysts; there is plenty of political geography to study by classical methods. There should be an effort, however, to realize what are the *principles* behind the major advanced mathematical processes, and a willingness to study the conclusions of studies which use them. Understanding will be improved if discussions are held with students experienced in mathematical analysis; especially if their help is solicited in problems which may be amenable to their skills. If papers with a mathematical bias are incomprehensible to the traditional geographer they should not hesitate to write to the author requesting clarification; I have yet to meet an academic who did not respond to an interest in his work.

It follows from the preceding remarks, that the mathematical political geographer should phrase his conclusions in language which will be understood by the widest possible audience. If such authors are in the habit of sending manuscripts to colleagues for criticism prior to publication, it might be wise to include a known traditionalist, in order to test the clarity of the conclusions to such people. It is also essential that geographers expert in mathematical techniques should be vigilant, so that papers which are unhelpful or wrong can be identified and exposed. There is so much ignorance of mathematical techniques, that there is a real danger that some papers will appear to be sound to the untutored. If papers which simply use a technique for the sake of using it, or which fail to meet the very rigorous standards demanded by the technique in its original discipline, are not identified and criticized by geographers, the subject will be set back unnecessarily if the exposure is made by a scholar from another discipline.

It is also important that the mathematical techniques should be shown to work, and experts in this field should be urged to press ahead with analyses of those subjects which will yield the fastest results. For all the mathematical analyses of elections in the past decade none of the scholars concerned has yet produced a work which compares with Goguel's analysis of the French elections or Pelling's survey of British election results. This probably means that political geographers would be better advised to concentrate on those subjects where nominal measurements are available at the expense of those situations where ordinal measurements must be used. For example, in January 1970 I constructed a table which showed, in a descriptive fashion, the characteristics of areas which had harboured secessionist movements around the world in the period 1960–70. An enthusiastic student asked me to assign values on a five-point scale to these qualities, so that he could carry out a mathematical analysis of the subject. Predictably the results were disappointing, and perhaps, more importantly, there is no guarantee that if I had to assign values to those characteristics again I would give the same figures. Political geographers would be well advised to avoid mathematical analysis of subjects like this.

3 Frontiers and boundaries

Frontiers and boundaries are respectively the zones and lines which separate areas of different political authority. Political geographers have studied both features in detail since political areal variation is often pronounced in their vicinity. Boundaries and frontiers are evocative subjects, which easily arouse patriotic or nationalist feelings, and Siegfried has warned of the inherent dangers in such topics.

> Le sujet (les frontières), avouons-le, est dangéreux pour un savant, car il est tout pénétré de passions politiques, tout encombrés d'arrière-pensées. Le gens ont trop d'intérêts en jeu, quand ils parlent de frontières, pour en parler de sang-froid: le malentendu est permanent. (Siegfried 1938, vii)

Although this distinguished political geographer was writing at a time when fierce political passions were being aroused in Europe over boundaries, he was correct in stating that the problem was permanent. In recent years some scholars have apparently been unable to take a detached view of the boundary disputes between India and China, India and Pakistan and Israel and its Arab neighbours. Nor is it only international boundaries which provoke strong sentiments, many proposals to alter internal administrative boundaries have aroused fierce local opposition.

Boundaries are the focus of practical concern for politicians, surveyors, administrators and military leaders and it would be unsound for such people to take a detached view of something which vitally concerns them and the people they serve. Politicians know that boundaries are sensitive subjects in international relations, and that apparent threats against the state's boundaries can be a powerful force for political cohesion. Surveyors are aware of the problems of marking lines on the ground and they are interested in reducing the difficulties of finding and maintaining such lines. Administrators recognize that boundaries delimit the area within which they exercise authority and that the ease of their tasks will vary with the particular boundary selected. Military leaders are concerned with the problems of attack and defence, and understand that different boundaries alter these problems. Appropriately enough, it is the persons who have a practical interest in boundaries, who decide where international and intra-national boundaries will lie. The scholar can afford to take a detached view of boundaries which are known to have originated through the interaction of the subjective opinions and desires of interested parties. It is always possible that objective analyses of boundaries will contain much that is of interest and value to people concerned with boundaries in a practical way; but there always must be much material which is of no practical significance, so scholars should not be disappointed if their studies do not seem to receive the attention from non-academics which they think is merited.

In fact the work of geographers on boundaries is fairly well known by other scholars and practical men, and it is doubtful if any other academic field has contributed as much to boundary studies. Writings by political scientists such as Kapil (1968) which repeat many common errors about 'good and bad boundaries' and about the ease of finding astronomic boundaries, and ignore most recent studies by geographers, are fortunately rare.

The political geographer's interest in boundaries and frontiers was defined in an earlier work in the following terms:

> There are two aspects of boundary and frontier studies which are of interest to geographers, whether engaged in topical or regional studies. First, the position and character of any boundary or frontier is the resultant of the interaction of many factors, some of which are geographical, and best studied by geographers. Second, once any boundary or frontier is established it is capable of influencing the landscape of which it is a part and the development and policies of the separated states. This aspect is also a legitimate field of geographic inquiry. (Prescott 1967, 28–9)

It is important to make explicit a point which is left implicit in this statement. The influence of geographical and other factors on the position and character of any boundary must be exerted through individuals of both countries concerned; similarly, the boundary can only influence the landscape by influencing the thoughts and actions of individuals concerned with administering or living in the borderland. In short, the geographical study of boundaries and frontiers is very much concerned with human behaviour in two distinct areas. Firstly, there is the behaviour of national governments towards each other; such behaviour will determine the evolution of the boundary and frontier, the character of disputes associated with the boundary, and the formulation of regulations to cover intercourse between the two states. Secondly, there is the behaviour of individuals who live in the borderland or near the frontier. Their perception of the boundary, and the framework of government regulations, will influence their economic activities and the ease with which they can communicate with trans-border regions. It must be recognized that often it will be necessary to study such citizens in an aggregate fashion.

To these behavioural approaches to boundaries and frontiers the political geographer must add the systematic study of the boundary, borderland and frontier. Indeed, such systematic studies will generally precede any examination of boundaries and frontiers and national or individual behaviour. The remainder of this chapter examines the systematic and behavioural approaches to studies of frontiers and boundaries separately. The separation seems worth while even though it is recognized that frontiers and boundaries form a political continuum through time, since boundaries usually evolve from frontiers. The distinction is made here for two reasons. Firstly, political frontiers between states are rare today; they have generally been exchanged for boundaries, the last transfer occurring in the Arabian peninsula. In some situations there are *de facto* frontiers between states with conflicting claims. For example, prior to the Sino-Indian hostilities in 1962, the uncontrolled territory between the two states might have been considered a practical frontier, although both states concerned would reject this interpretation. Political frontiers might also be considered to exist in countries such as South Vietnam, where there are uncertain areas which are not under the control of either the official government or the rebel armies. Secondly, geographers have made many more studies of boundaries than frontiers, and it seems sensible to include the few frontier studies which exist in one place. It is difficult to explain completely the apparent neglect of frontiers by political geographers. Contributory causes must include the absence of contemporary political frontiers, the greater availability of documents relating to boundaries, and the greater ease with which fieldwork can be done in boundary studies.

Since frontiers normally precede boundaries in development they will be considered first.

The systematic study of frontiers

There are two main types of frontiers. *Political frontiers* separate individual states, while *settlement frontiers* separate the developed and undeveloped areas of a single state. Settlement frontiers can be further subdivided into primary and secondary types. Primary settlement frontiers no longer exist; they occurred when a government and people gradually extended their influence and occupation over an area to which they had some form of legal title. Thus the American frontier, advancing westwards through the United States and Canada was the most famous primary settlement frontier. These frontiers marked the *de facto* limit of the government's authority and their movements were often irregular and unplanned; similarly the economic activities and population densities associated with them showed a wide variation. By contrast secondary settlement frontiers occur in many states today; they border the areas which have not been developed because of adverse physical characteristics or inadequate techniques to exploit them. The authority of states extends beyond secondary settlement frontiers, and their advance is usually through carefully planned programmes involving government support; the population densities of such zones are generally low, except in some parts of South-East Asia, and the economic activities normally fall within a narrow range of extensive farming and mining.

The information which a systematic study of political frontiers should provide relates to the width and position of the frontier, the extent to which it is marked by defensive walls, ditches or palisades, its physical nature, the density, distribution and cultural characteristics of the people living in and near the frontier, and economic activities associated with the frontiers and adjoining areas. It will rarely be possible to accumulate this information through fieldwork since the frontiers no longer exist. The major exception will occur where features such as the Great Wall of China and the Roman Wall were built to mark the edge of the political frontier. Useful fieldwork in such areas will normally require archaeological skills, and fortunately archaeologists have done much of this work and their descriptions and conclusions are readily available to geographers. (See for example Richmond 1966; Solway 1965; and Birley 1952.) Fieldwork is also possible in connection with those frontiers which existed most recently; such frontiers were found between tribal political units in Africa, South America and Asia during the nineteenth century. Fieldwork in such situations calls for skills developed by anthropologists and again the geographer is fortunate that so much of this material is readily available. For example, studies by Huntingford (1955), Bradbury (1957), Forde and Jones (1950), and Bohannan (1953) are invaluable in any study of indigenous frontiers in the area of Nigeria. Generally the information will have to be sought in secondary sources prepared by archaeologists, anthropologists, historians and historical geographers. Particular value must be attached to the reports which were prepared by persons who lived at the time the frontiers existed. These would include classical writers such as Tacitus in respect of ancient frontiers in Europe, travellers' accounts such as that by Nachtigal (1879) relating to West Africa, and correspondence in the archives of colonial powers in Europe and Asia, from officials who were concerned with the acquisition of territory.

The systematic accumulation of facts about primary settlement frontiers is usually less difficult than in the case of political frontiers. The best cases of such features existed during the last century in

Canada, the United States, southern Africa and Australia. The main facts which are required for the frontier at any particular time concern the location, the rate of advance or retreat, the distribution, numbers and cultural and economic qualities of the frontier's population, the physical nature of the region and the economic activities found there. Fieldwork will be possible in many areas, especially where the unfavable nature of the physical landscape has discouraged significant subsequent development. For example, it is still possible to obtain a very clear picture of the problems faced by frontiersmen moving through the Canadian Rocky Mountains, or into the Kalahari desert. There will often be a much richer store of secondary sources from which facts can be derived, including many contemporary accounts and newspapers, for the frontier period is acknowledged by many to have been important in fashioning a national identity. In addition the volume of official sources will usually be much larger in respect of primary settlement frontiers than in respect of political frontiers.

Only when the catalogue of facts about the various kinds of frontiers has been established for a series of consecutive and relevant time sections, will it be possible to proceed to dynamic behavioural analysis.

The behavioural analysis of frontiers

The behaviour of states towards others lying beyond the political frontier is the first type to be considered. This behaviour will determine the use which is made of the frontier. Clearly these uses will vary, and often there will not be any formal agreement by the states concerned. For example, Tilho (1910, 362) has recorded that the armies of both Sokoto and Bornu raided into the frontier to capture Bedde pagans as slaves, by agreement. In other cases casual grazing rights have been permitted by flanking states. Some frontiers, in direct contrast, were preserved as unpopulated areas to reduce the chance of friction and to make it easy to identify enemies. Huntingford (1955) has described how some frontiers in the Horn of Africa were peopled by fierce brigands who were encouraged by the flanking states so that it would be difficult for enemies to attack and for slaves to escape.

History provides many examples of changes in the relative strength of states, causing alterations in the width and position of frontiers. Boundaries are much less susceptible to change in position as the relative powers of states fluctuate. The existence of uncontrolled land on the borders of the state would always represent a temptation to expand, if this could be done without exciting opposition which could prove dangerous. Encroachment by one or both sides into the frontier could occur for a number of reasons. The existence of severe overpopulation, or the failure of crops, or the availability of new techniques to use the frontier's resources could explain the incorporation of new areas by some states. Kelly (1969) has shown how food shortages encouraged the Inca Empire to extend eastwards into empty, forest areas, and southwards into areas where Inca farming techniques would enable richer production than that achieved by the local population. In some cases frontier zones were invaded to compensate the state for land lost elsewhere. The wave-like motions of some African migrations in the west and south, are well known, and have been clearly recorded by Oliver and Atmore (1967). Some advances into the frontier were made for strategic reasons. East (1962) has shown how the Roman legions advanced into Noricum and Pannonia in order to protect the eastern flank of Gaul; Lattimore (1962, 171) has described how Chinese armies invaded the frontier in order to break-up threatening concentrations of tribal power. It is important to stress that the behaviour of any state towards the frontier and adjacent states would not only depend on the economic and political situations mentioned above; the physical nature of the frontier would also be significant. Unless there were over-riding political, economic, or strategic factors, hostile environments of marsh, high mountains and deserts would discourage annexation, while favourable environments such as grasslands and woodlands would encourage it. Lattimore (1962, 476) notes the significance of the different frontier environments to the north and south of China.

Annexation is not the only type of state behaviour which would alter the size and position of frontiers. Flanking states may dispose of all or part of the frontier by creating marches, or buffer states, or identifying spheres of interest or influence. Marches are areas of the frontier organized on semi-permanent military lines to defend the state. Charlemagne established marches to defend his empire and some of them became autonomous states (Curzon 1907, 27). The term buffer state refers to a state created, or allowed to exist, by two or more powerful neighbours so that their territorial contact will be avoided. Marshall-Cornwall (1935) has described many such territories in Asia, such as Thailand, Sikkim and Afghanistan. Spheres of interest and influence are territorial arrangements reached by states to reserve freedom of action, generally without responsibility and without competition from other states. Such arrangements were common in Africa and Asia during the last century; in modern times they usually refer to the so-called satellite state of the major powers.

Individual behaviour of frontiersmen has been influenced by government regulations and their perception of the possibilities offered by the frontier. Most of the regulations have related to the defence of the state. Lattimore (1940) has shown that the Great Wall of China was designed to reduce the opportunities for Chinese living in the area to become assimilated with the barbarians and thus pose a threat to the

Chinese state. Lattimore (1962, 112) describes how 100,000 Chinese colonists were introduced into the area of Ninghsia to counter threats from the Hsiungnu in 127 B.C. Such colonists were expected to provide military assistance in time of need; this requirement was also made of the Roman farmers near Hadrian's Wall. Wiens (1969) has described how the Manchu Emperor in 1755 compelled Kalmuk tribes to resettle in a scattered fashion among other tribes in the frontier in order to reduce the chance of further conflict. He also notes that the Manchus built nine walled fortress cities in the Ili valley, and sixteen similar cities in other areas of the frontier.

Geographers have not been much concerned with the behaviour of the individual frontiersman. Kristof, a political scientist, has characterized frontiers in the following terms:

> Frontiers are a characteristic of rudimentary socio-political relations, relations marked by rebelliousness, lawlessness, and/or absence of laws. (Kristof 1959, 281)

It follows that the people who would thrive in such circumstances would be those who were self-reliant, and capable of improvisation. It would be surprising if investigation of individual and aggregate behaviour of frontiersmen did not show that the environment influenced economic activities, building styles, and the distribution of settlements and routes. The problem of such studies is that they would have to be based on historical studies since there are no political frontiers remaining. Comparison with the behaviour of individuals living close to disputed zones today is unlikely to be helpful, because of the rapid means of communication which are available now.

Turning now to behaviour associated with primary settlement frontiers the behaviour of the advancing state to the political organisation in its path is very important. In North America, southern Africa and Australia the advancing state enjoyed technical superiority over the indigenous groups that lived beyond the frontier. Any state faced with the problem of advancing a primary settlement frontier into occupied country can adopt one or both of two policies. Firstly, the indigenous population could be killed or driven beyond the state's borders. Secondly, the indigenous population could be absorbed into the state in one of two ways; either they could be accepted as citizens with equal rights, or they could be restricted to particular areas. The policy selected will depend on many factors, two of which will be the numbers and political organization of the indigenous population and the nature of their environment. The large population and efficient military organization of the Zulus and some other African tribes encouraged the authorities in what is now South Africa and Rhodesia to by-pass these areas and eventually constitute them into reserves or homelands. The small number of aborigines in Tasmania and the fact that some of them occupied land suitable for European settlement made it more likely that this group would be killed or driven off the land without much concern for creating reserves. In Southwest Africa the Bushmen, who occupied unattractive desert country were left almost undisturbed for many years by the German administrators. The behaviour of the indigenous population is also important in influencing the rate at which the settlement frontier advances. Where resistance is offered, especially in difficult terrain, the advance may be turned into a retreat, or a period of stagnation may occur. Such factors are important because the rate at which the frontier advances will often influence the type of landscape which results. Clarke (1959) has noted that slow advance results in closer more orderly settlement than rapid advance.

The behaviour of the state towards the actual frontier area and the citizens living there is the second important aspect to be considered. In the classical case of the North American frontier it is noticeable that as the frontier rolled across the continent, administration on the frontier became more efficient. This was the result of increasing experience with mining and land laws, and improved technology relating to communications and warfare. The main aspects of government regulations of interest to the geographer will deal with land settlement and economic activities; historians have published much of interest in this field (Turner 1953; Clarke 1959; Billington 1959).

Geographers have paid as little attention to the behaviour of frontiersmen on primary settlement frontiers as they have to those on political frontiers; the field has been left mainly to historians. Initial profitable lines of study would probably include identification of the motives which encouraged individuals to move to the frontier. These motives will include an amalgam of pressures, represented by unfavourable social, economic and political conditions in the homeland, and attractions, represented by opportunities for individual economic, social and political gains.

Since the systematic study of boundaries has been fully covered in available texts (Jones 1945; Dorion 1963; and Prescott 1967), it is proposed to proceed to the behavioural analysis of boundaries.

The behavioural analysis of boundaries

Two types of behaviour fall under this heading. Firstly, there is the behaviour of political authorities to each other. Such authorities will include national governments and sub-national administrations, thus both internal and international boundaries will be involved. The way in which international and internal boundaries influence individual behaviour is the second section of this study.

In each of these types the political geographer should focus on three principal aspects. Firstly, the geographical aims and motives of governments and individuals should be isolated. Secondly, the influence of geographical factors on the selection of a particular course of action and the outcome of that action must be determined. Finally, the geographical results of this administrative or individual behaviour should be assessed. In each case, the nouns *aim*, *factors* and *result* have been qualified by the adjective *geographical*. No attempt is made here to distinguish geographical aims, factors or results from other kinds. In each case individual geographers must decide how far they wish to pursue the inquiry. For example, all geographers would consider the desire for territory for strategic purposes to be a geographical aim; many would not consider the initiation of a dispute to embarrass a neighbouring government to be a geographical aim. All geographers would consider the geographical knowledge of one of the principal boundary negotiators to be a geographical factor; few would be interested in assessing the significance of the personality of one of the principal negotiators to the success of the talks. All geographers would consider the development of new settlement patterns after the transfer of territory from one authority to another as being a geographical result; few would examine the consequences on the cultural trends in a country of the inclusion of a new ethnic group by boundary change. If those who continually work on the remote frontiers of geography can demonstrate the validity of their work they will be followed by growing numbers of colleagues; otherwise these pioneers will be assimilated by the social psychologists and other social scientists. Reynolds and McNulty (1968, 26) who seek to advance the frontiers of geography recommend an approach to the study of patterns of individual behaviour which examines the relevant processes generating those patterns. Many geographers will be content to leave the investigation of such processes to social psychologists and concentrate instead on the results of established aggregate behaviour patterns. There is room in political geography for both approaches, and they will generally show their greatest divergence in the field of individual behaviour where the numbers involved make some consideration of both individual and aggregate patterns possible. In the case of behaviour by governments, the number of appropriate cases is much smaller and aggregate generalization comparing governments may be dangerous. However, it is often impossible to identify the role of a single member of government, and therefore government behaviour will usually be investigated as the aggregate behaviour of the individuals who are members.

Looking at the behaviour of states to each other there are three main areas which need attention. Firstly, there is the behaviour of states revealed during the evolution of a common boundary. Secondly, there is the behaviour of governments during disputes associated with boundaries. In many cases disputes will arise during the evolution of the boundary, but they may also develop long after the boundary is apparently settled. Thirdly, the state functions which are applied at international boundaries exhibit the nature of administrative behaviour to other states as well as to the citizens of the country applying the functions.

Looking at boundary evolution, a useful distinction has been made by Lapradelle (1928) and Jones (1945), between the stages of international boundary formation. The first stage of *allocation* concerns the simple political division of territory, and gives the first general shape to the states involved. Straight lines connecting known geographical features such as mountains and the sources of rivers or waterfalls, or coordinates of latitude and longitude are common characteristics of such boundaries. These lines would usually be refined during the stage of *delimitation*. This involves the selection of a specific boundary site which would require detailed geographical knowledge not available when the allocation was made. The final stage of boundary development is called *demarcation*; this requires that the boundary should be marked on the ground by any appropriate means including pillars, cleared vistas and fences.

Not all boundaries will pass through all these stages. In some situations the boundary which allocates territory will never be delimited. The lines of latitude and longitude which exist today as international boundaries survive for a variety of reasons. In some cases the flanking states have never been able to agree on another line more closely related to the landscape; in others the line traverses through unattractive deserts which the states concerned have no present intention of developing. In East Africa straight boundaries were preserved between Kenya and Tanganyika because both were under British administration. In certain circumstances, especially when the boundary is drawn in the light of comprehensive geographical knowledge, it may be possible to select a boundary site immediately and there will be no stage of allocation. Lastly, in many cases once boundaries have been delimited their demarcation may be considered unnecessary because of the inhospitable nature of the terrain, or because of the expense which would be involved. Equivalent stages could be established for some federal boundaries, but internal boundaries often evolve in a haphazard manner, and few of them are demarcated.

As the international boundary passes through the stages of allocation, delimitation and demarcation, its definition may become increasingly precise and the location of the boundary may alter. Since disputes will often find their source in faulty definitions or objections to particular locations, and since the location of the boundary must be known in assessing the influence which it may have on national or individual behaviour, it is important that any political geographer should know the life history of any boundary he is studying in terms of definition and position.

States will seek to create boundaries out of frontiers to satisfy a wide range of aims. In some cases there will be a desire to remove a confused administrative position resulting from uncertainty in jurisdiction. Gradually the neutral areas between countries have been eradicated, the latest to vanish separated Kuwait and Saudi Arabia (*The Geographer*, 1970, No. 103). The unresolved dispute over El Chamizal plagued American and Mexican administrations until the agreement of 1965 (Hill 1965). Boundary negotiations are often initiated by states which seek to secure title to an area which appears strategically or commercially important. Under the Franco-German protocol of 1885 which defined a line between Kamerun and French Congo, the German Emperor engaged to abstain from all political action south of the line, while the French Government renounced all its claims and pretensions to territory north of the line and also engaged to abstain from political activities in that area. The desire here was to pre-empt territory which might turn out to be valuable. In some cases boundary negotiations have been used to secure peace, either between two states of equivalent power, such as Britain and France, whose posts in Borgu were interlocked in 1897, or between unequal powers such as Mexico and the United States in 1848, when Mexico was anxious to negotiate before American armies swept through the entire territory of the state. Boundary negotiations were used by France in 1911 to win German recognition of the French presence in Morocco. The negotiations were in respect of the boundary between Kamerun and the French area of Chad, and resulted in Germany being granted 100,000 square miles of former French territory. Clearly different stages of boundary evolution would be involved in these differing aims. The desire to pre-empt territory could easily be satisfied by a line allocating territory; the need for a boundary which removed administrative confusion between two states might well require a demarcated line.

Many kinds of geographical factor will influence the evolution of boundaries in different ways. Perhaps the state of geographical knowledge should be placed first. The attitude of any negotiator will depend on his perception of the landscape through which the boundary is to be drawn. In present times with rapid map production through air photographs there is little excuse for the negotiator to have an impression which is significantly different from the real situation. But until the Second World War the information available to governments was often incomplete, and during the last century, when so many of the boundaries of Asia, Africa and South America were decided, information was often extremely inaccurate. Kleber (1968) records how Lord Baltimore mistakenly assumed that Cape Henlopen, the terminus of the boundary between Maryland and Pennsylvania, was twenty miles south of the mouth of the Delaware River, because it was shown in this place on a map provided years before by his agent. In fact the Cape was at the mouth of the river. If the agreement had specified the Cape his lordship would have profited, but the agreement referred to the point twenty miles south of the river. The increasing precision of boundary definitions during the last century reflected the growing geographical knowledge about borderlands.

If we assume perfect geographical knowledge about the borderland it must then be realized that any element in that landscape may be the crucial factor for a particular section of boundary. The distribution of people, of different ethnic groups, of mountains and rivers, of mineral deposits, of routes and even of places with an emotional importance for the state may be the main factor which most influences the desire of a particular government for a particular boundary. For example, the Indian Government places great emphasis on the watershed principle in its negotiations with China concerning the Himalayan border; in 1926 certain areas of Uganda were ceded to the Anglo-Egyptian Sudan to re-unite certain tribal groups; the discovery of oil in the Neutral Zone between Kuwait and Saudi Arabia in 1938, led eventually to the partition of the area in 1965; and Hartshorne (1950) has shown that the existence of certain German cemeteries was a significant factor in determining the 1871 boundary in France. In 1898 France tried to persuade Britain to yield Illo on the Niger because a French soldier was buried there. The British Government rejected the request, perhaps because Lugard told them that the Frenchman was the victim of a jealous husband in a *crime passionel* (Perham and Bull 1962, 384).

It is also essential to be aware that non-geographical factors might be decisive in changing the course of boundary negotiations. Perhaps the best example concerns the incorrect decoding of a telegram in Lagos in 1916 which cost Britain the eastern half of German Bornu.

The significant factors will also vary with the stage of boundary evolution. In the stage of allocation, factors related to general strategy, which may be described as large scale, will be important; in the stage of demarcation the small scale issues of farm boundaries and clear turning points will be decisive in moving the boundary a few hundred metres one way or the other. During the stage of delimitation the crucial arguments may relate to both large and small scale factors and shifts in position may also be considerable or slight.

The possible results of boundary evolution will also be varied. In some cases the establishment of boundaries will allow the orderly settlement of borderlands, in others movements of boundaries will be followed by the migration of people who have been transferred from one country to another. If people transferred from one side of the boundary to the other by a new treaty do not emigrate, they may form an irredentist movement, which will create problems for the government concerned. This was the situation which Ethiopia faced due to Somali nationalism in the post-independence period. There is always the possibility that if the boundary lies through an unoccupied, inhospitable area, without attractive resources, that there will be no geographical consequences following the establishment of the boundary.

Characteristics of the behaviour of states to each other are also revealed by boundary disputes. Such disputes can be divided into four classes. Firstly, there are those disputes where a state lays claim to land or territorial waters belonging to another state, and these are called *territorial disputes*. Secondly, there are disputes over discrepancies between the definition of the boundary and the boundary demarcation, and these are called *positional disputes*. The state initiating territorial or positional disputes is seeking an alteration in the position of the boundary, either to acquire certain areas or to make the demarcated line coincide with the defined line. The third kind of dispute relates to the functions applied at the boundary by states. The recurring complaints by the Bonn Government against the restrictions on travel to West Berlin raised by the Government of East Germany provides the best contemporary example of such *functional disputes*. Fourthly, an increasing number of disputes concerns the use of some resource which spans the boundary, such as a river, oyster bed or oilfield. These are called *resource disputes*. Any state which initiates a boundary dispute of any kind is seeking to gain some advantage. In some cases the advantage sought is permanent and tangible. For example, Israel raised the thorny problem of an agreement concerning the use of the Jordan waters so that the agricultural economy of the state could be strengthened, so that more settlers could be accommodated in Israel, and so that certain lightly populated areas could be more intensively settled. Arab intransigence in this matter naturally sought to deny these advantages to Israel. In the same way, if Morocco succeeds in its claims to Spanish Sahara, it will benefit from control of the enormous phosphate deposits located there. These tangible advantages may concern either the economic or strategic strength of the state. Additional territories may include new resources for industry and agriculture not previously available, and may provide a more secure routeway for trade with the outside world. Transit rights for a landlocked state won in a functional dispute may improve the cost structure of imports and exports, and relieve dependence on a single neighbour. Agreements over a common river may enable its use for the generation of electricity or the irrigation of farmland. The new territory may also have an intrinsic strategic value. If Israel is able to retain the Golan Heights it will be more secure from any future Syrian attack; the McMahon Line gives India a much easier border to defend against China than a boundary along the foothills north of the Brahmaputra plain.

There are also intangible benefits which may be obtained from initiating a boundary dispute. If a positional dispute is satisfactorily resolved the risk of friction along the common boundary should be reduced. In some cases boundary disputes are initiated for political reasons. During their periods in office both President Nkrumah and President Sukarno used border disputes against Togo and Malaysia respectively to distract attention from domestic economic problems. In 1963 the Philippine's claim to North Borneo (now Sabah) was designed to hinder the incorporation of the area into the Malaysian Federation. Some extravagant territorial claims have been used as a *casus belli*.

While the examples used above all concern national authorities it must be remembered that sub-national authorities will also engage in boundary disputes. In the United States several federal States engage in disputes over the position of their boundaries. Bowden (1959), Chapman (1949) and Andrew (1949) have all written on various boundary disputes involving Texas and its neighbours. Even local government authorities have been known to engage in disputes over their boundaries. Their motives in such cases are usually connected with increased economic wealth and the resolution of planning problems.

The political geographer should be aware of five factors which will influence the outcome of any boundary dispute and which he may properly consider. Firstly, the geographical importance of the dispute to one or both governments will influence their attitude to the question. For example, the Chinese claim to areas of eastern Russia is not vital to the existence of the Chinese state; the country can thrive and prosper within its present borders. Indeed, the dispute has more ideological than geographical significance to China. There are many similar claims in South America which have hung fire for decades. Conversely, Iran's claim to a median boundary with Iraq in the Shatt el Arab is of vital importance to Iran. Ships visiting Iran's major port, Abadan, have to use Iraq's territorial waters, and from time to time Iraq has interfered with such passage. If this connection was ever severed Iran's trade would be strangled. This fact explains Iran's determined stand on this dispute which has been considered by Melamid (1968) and Sevian (1968).

Secondly, the outcome of the dispute will be influenced by the extent to which both authorities can derive some benefit. For example, the resource dispute between Kuwait and Saudi Arabia over the petroleum deposit in the Neutral Zone did not prove too difficult because both countries could share the potential wealth. This generalization would also apply to the use of boundary waters between Victoria in Canada and Washington in the United States. Conversely, where the dispute concerns the possession of a particular area it will be difficult to find common benefits. If Austria succeeded in its claim to the Italian Tyrol, then its improved economic and strategic position would be at the expense of Italy. In the last century, the one-sided nature of some boundary movements was recognized by territorial exchanges in widely separated areas by the colonial powers. France and Britain made a treaty which referred to both Nigeria and Newfoundland. In some cases the line has been moved in opposite directions in different sectors so that both sides gain and lose territory, while in others the government gaining a firm territorial title has paid a sum of money to the state making the concession. A variation on this theme was provided recently by the Algerian–Moroccan agreement of May 1970. In return for Moroccan recognition of a line west of Colomb-Bechar and Tindouf, which leaves the iron ore deposits of Gara-Djebilet in Algeria, Algeria has given the Moroccan Government a share in the exploitation of the iron-ore mines. The resolution of positional disputes which involve only short distances will often be welcomed by friendly governments which prefer a clear unambiguous line to one which may promote friction.

Thirdly, the relative strengths of the countries will influence the outcome of any dispute. Where those strengths are approximately equivalent this factor will not be decisive, but where one state is recognizably stronger than another, the claims of the stronger state are likely to prevail. The boundary movements in favour of Germany at the expense of Czechoslovakia before the Second World War, those in favour of Russia at the expense of Finland in 1940, and the readiness with which Burma, Nepal and Afghanistan agreed to new treaties with China in 1960, 1961 and 1963 respectively, all owed something to the much greater strength of one of the parties to the negotiations. Normally countries will not attempt to assert claims regarding boundaries against stronger neighbours. Such claims are held in abeyance until some opportune moment, and it is noticeable when powerful states are in decline, as Germany was in 1919 and 1945, and as Turkey was at the beginning of this century, that small countries quickly make their boundary claims known.

The fourth factor involves what may be described as the world political climate. In the last century military force was accepted as one of the ways of settling boundary disputes. In recent decades many governments have expressed disapproval of such behaviour. This disapproval has been shown by the resolutions of the Organization of African Unity in respect of the border conflicts between the Somali Republic and Kenya and Ethiopia, and between Algeria and Morocco, and by the resolutions of the United Nations Security Council in respect of advances by Israel into Arab territory. Some important territorial disputes involving Britain and Iceland, Cambodia and Thailand, and India and Pakistan have been settled since the Second World War by legal processes, and this is a trend which has been increasingly evident during the present century. Cukwurah (1967) lists over a hundred cases involving international and federal boundaries. Where these legal processes are followed the fifth factor will apply; it concerns the merits of the arguments advanced by the contending powers. Unless the matter is being adjudicated the merits of the rival arguments are not likely to be decisive. In non-legal situations their main role will be to boost domestic morale and solicit international support; any final decisions taken will probably be based on self-interest and political expediency. The arguments which are advanced either in court or during negotiations fall into two groups first described by Hill (1945). Legal arguments aver that the claimant state should possess certain territory, or certain privileges regarding transit or resources, or that the interpretation of the boundary definition by the claimant state is correct. The second category of arguments indicates that while the claimant state has no legal right to enforce its view, it would be appropriate if its arguments, founded in geography, history, economics, ethnology and strategy, held sway.

Most legal arguments lie outside the province of the political geographer, although any geographer interested in boundary disputes should be familiar with the legal bases of claims to territory. Governments have tried to base legal arguments on so-called principles of hinterlands and effective occupation in Africa, and the sector theory in Antarctica, but the standard legal claims are based on formal treaties, and in the principles of *uti possidetis* and prescription. *Uti possidetis* is the principle under which the states of South America succeeded the colonial empires, and means that the new states were coterminous with the previous colonies. Such a declaration ensured that no other countries claimed territory lying between any two states. Unfortunately the principle can be interpreted in two ways. It can either mean that the legal colonial boundaries become the limits of the new states, or it can mean that the practical administrative boundaries of colonial empires become the framework of the new nations. The *de jure* and *de facto* boundaries did not always coincide. Prescription refers to the uninterrupted occupation of an area by a single authority, perhaps without any formal treaty being concluded. This principle forms part of the Indian case against China in the Aksai Chin.

The most common geographical arguments suggest that the boundary should coincide with some prominent physical feature to avoid confusion, or that some divided area really has a basic geographical unity. The first set of arguments is a remnant of the old-fashioned ideas about natural boundaries, which today have no academic currency. Their worthlessness has been demonstrated by a generation of political geographers since Fawcett (1918). It is now recognized that boundaries following mountain crests, watersheds and rivers have no greater intrinsic value than other lines in separating friendly states. The boundary should be drawn on the basis of greatest convenience and benefit to both sides, wherever it might lie. In using geographical arguments to demonstrate the unity of areas which have been divided, or which are in danger of being divided, many different regional qualities may be considered, since these overlap with the categories of economic and ethnic arguments mentioned earlier, they can all be considered together. After the First World War Rumania claimed the Banat area because of the complementary labour shortages on the plains and the unemployment problems of the adjoining hills. Part of the claim by the Somali Republic against Ethiopia to the Haud and Ogaden areas, rests on the use which migrant Somali herds make of these areas for summer pastures. Pounds (1963, 239–44) has provided an interesting account of claims by states for access to the sea, which is a particular form of economic argument in favour of boundary change. German insistence on the curious extension of Southwest Africa, and the strip of territory linking lake Tanganyika and lake Edward leased by Belgium to Britain under the Agreement of 1894, are also examples of the importance of transit consideration in boundary disputes.

Claims to territory on ethnic grounds form a very important proportion of all claims. The boundaries of Europe after 1918 were largely fashioned in accordance with the patterns of language in the borderlands. The post-colonial disputes between Afghanistan and Pakistan, between the Somali Republic and its neighbours, between Nigeria and Cameroun, between Ghana and Togo, and between Nigeria and Dahomey are all based on the division of ethnic groups by international boundaries. Ethnic disputes have often been solved either by moving the boundary or expelling the minority. In the case of the disputes between the Somali and Ethiopia and Kenya Republic a new alternative seems to have been tried, which is revealed in a speech by Prime Minister Egal of the Somali Republic.

> To start with our policy towards the Northern Frontier District of Kenya, we elicit an admission first that the case was open to debate, and secondly that until such time as a fully negotiated settlement could be reached we could have a say in its affairs and welfare. . . . We have a say in its administration, and there are close trade relations. Our currency is a recognised medium of exchange. . . . We are proud to point out that the odious burden of taxation has been lifted from these regions (Haud and Ogaden of Ethiopia) as a result of our

contacts with the Ethiopian authorities. The country is acknowledged to be within the sphere of our policy's influence; it is open to free commerce and the free movement of Somalis. (*Somali News*, 18th November 1970)

Apparently the political boundary has remained in position but it no longer operates as a complete barrier to the influence of the Somali Government.

Strategic claims to territory are also fairly common. The Soviet Union claimed Finnish territory in 1939 to reduce the vulnerability of Leningrad to artillery attack, and subsequently captured the requisite area in a brief war. German negotiators in 1871 gave prime consideration to the defensibility of certain sections of the boundary with France near Metz (Hartshorne, 1950).

Historical arguments in favour of boundary change are also common, and usually represent the efforts of a state to regain territory which was lost in an earlier period. Spanish claims to Gibraltar, and Turkish claims to Cyprus are representative of such claims. Frequently these arguments are used to bolster other parts of the case. The strongest historical arguments are those which refer to a period not long past such as the claims by Czechoslovakia and Poland against Germany in 1945, and the claims by Cambodia against Thailand in 1946. The demands for the return of those parts of China lost to Russia in 1860, and the claims of Morocco to Mauretania and Spanish Sahara are too deeply imbedded in history to be seriously considered today, on those grounds alone.

Geographical arguments are very important in positional disputes which usually arise because some part of the definition used ambiguous terms, incorrect place names, non-existent points and contradictory definitions. The literature is full of cases of all those points, and some of it has been reviewed in an earlier study (Prescott 1967, 70–2). An excellent recent article, not included in that survey, was prepared by Adejuyigbe (1970); it deals with inaccurate definitions of the internal boundary between Ife and Ijesa in 1913 and 1932. He shows that both these definitions are riddled with inaccuracies and concludes by listing a set of sensible steps by which the problem may be solved.

The geographical results of any boundary dispute will obviously be related to which type of dispute is involved and the ability of the two sides to reach agreement. Boundary movement may take place in solving territorial and positional disputes, and the consequences of such movement would be the same as boundary movements recorded in the section dealing with boundary evolution. In some cases the territorial dispute may be eased by reducing the state functions applied at the boundary as in the Somali–Ethiopian dispute. If the dispute is not solved there will be two general situations. Firstly the geographical patterns of trade and settlement may continue unaltered. Secondly, there may be friction between the states which results in the stricter application of state functions at the boundary and the severance of trade. The Finnish–Soviet Union war followed the refusal of Finland to accede to Soviet demands; the nomadic Powindas of Afghanistan were prevented from entering Pakistan with their herds during the height of the Paktunistan dispute; and the Ghanaian–Togo border was closed after Togo had refused to give way on the Ewe issue (Hodder 1968). If resource disputes are solved there is likely to be economic development by at least one and possibly both countries involved. A good example of this is shown by the spurt in dam building on the Columbia River after the 1961 agreement between Canada and the United States. The resolution of functional disputes which normally concern boundary traffic will usually be followed by an increase in the flow of goods, people or capital across the boundary where restrictions have been eased. If a serious functional dispute remains unsolved the state initiating the dispute may try to find alternative routes to achieve its purposes. For example, when Mali was prevented from conducting trade through Dakar by Senegalese restrictions, the Government of Mali arranged an alternative route through the Ivory Coast. This new route has been preserved despite the resumption of good relations between Mali and Senegal.

In contrast with the considerable number of studies by geographers dealing with the evolution of boundaries and disputes associated with them there is a paucity of studies dealing with state functions applied at the boundary. This was my view in 1965 (Prescott 1967, 77) and a survey of subsequent literature shows that the position has not altered. The boundary itself has only one function, and this is to delimit the area within which authority is exercised. However, governments find it convenient to exercise many of their functions dealing with immigration, trade and health at the boundary. It is suggested here that political geographers can gain a valuable insight into the behaviour of states towards different neighbours by comparing the functions applied at each sector, and the manner in which they are operated. The point was driven home to me in 1960. On the Ghana–Togo border I was detained on suspicion of gun-running for President Nkrumah; two days later when I left northern Togo to enter Dahomey, each page of my passport was carefully examined by the officer who held it upside down the whole time! Studies of this nature can be supplemented by calculations of interactance in the style of Lösch (1954) and Mackay (1958).

The second major aspect of the behavioural study of boundaries concerns the behaviour of individuals living in the borderland. The framework for understanding this behaviour has two principal elements.

First, there are the regulations regarding the boundary and borderland laid down by the governments concerned. Initially these regulations tell us more about the behaviour and attitudes of governments than about individual behaviour, but they will apply whether they are perceived by the individual or not. Whether or not individuals understand customs regulations they are likely to be prevented from carrying contraband across the boundary if they cross at a customs post. The regulations which will most concern the political geographer relate to the number and location of crossing points, the types and volumes of merchandise which may be transported across the boundary, the qualifications of people allowed to cross the boundary, the ease with which money can be transferred from one side to another, and the extent to which people can settle close to the boundary. The marked contrast between boundaries where movement is completely controlled, as between East and West Germany, with boundaries where there are no controls, as between Niger and Nigeria, is obvious, but it should not be beyond the ingenuity of geographers to measure more subtle differences between boundary regulations. It would be a great advance if it was possible to compare the varying permeability of a single boundary in respect of people, goods, money and perhaps ideas, and then to extend that comparison to include other boundaries.

A few examples will show the importance of such studies. Daveau (1959) and Sevrin (1949) have shown how geographers should be aware of differences in exchange rates on opposite sides of the boundary as a factor influencing trade and economic developments in the borderland. There are many interesting cases where this investigation would be useful in Africa. An earlier quotation showed that Somali currency is recognized in the Ethiopian borderland: this contrasts with the situation in northern Botswana where the Zambian Kwacha is valueless, and in western Uganda where the Zaire (Congolese) franc is unacceptable. Kibulya (1967) has described the latter situation:

> The Uganda currency is readily accepted in Butalinga (Congo Democratic Republic) whereas the franc has no value in Bwamba. Hence there is more Uganda currency in Butalinga than Congolese money, whereas one could spend all his life in Bwamba without having ever seen a franc! Indeed the constant devaluation of the Congolese franc, especially after 1960 has been a great economic problem for the Batalinga . . . Undoubtedly economic and social developments have been deterred by this devaluation. (p. 51–2)

Kibulya also discusses the regulations regarding settlement and trade in some detail. The Congolese Government in 1967 allowed no settlement within two miles of the boundary with Uganda, thus the unoccupied area of Butalinga contrasted with the Ugandan region of

Bwamba, where there is a high density of population adjoining the boundary. Ugandan citizens visiting Zaire may not take any trade goods with them, but Zaire citizens can visit Ugandan markets freely and buy such commodities as they need. The intensification of government functions at the boundary can indicate changes in foreign policies, as the Spanish closure of the boundary with Gibraltar demonstrated.

The second element in the framework for understanding individual behaviour relates to the perception of the individual. Reynolds and McNulty (1968) have made the most useful consideration of this question. They clearly show the problems of relying too heavily on interactance studies in measuring aggregate behaviour, and they call for greater research into individual perception of the boundary as a barrier, which is linked to concepts of the subjective environment, and the action space of individuals which was suggested by Wolpert (1965). Aggregate analyses are excellent for understanding the results of individual behaviour, but less satisfactory in explaining why that behaviour occurred. For example, statistics will tell geographers how many people crossed particular boundaries in different directions, and perhaps even their ultimate destination, and these facts are very important in tracing geographical changes. But the statistics will not explain why these particular individuals migrated. These reasons can only be uncovered by personal inquiry among a sample population. Reynolds and McNulty suggest that the relevant processes generating patterns of individual behaviour should be studied, but some geographers will question this approach. While it is important to establish whether a person thinks that a nearby boundary is permeable or impermeable, since this will influence his behaviour, should the geographer press on to discover why this particular view is held. Research in this direction leads away from the core of political geography towards sociology and psychology, and this must sound a warning since there remains so much work undone at the heart of the subject.

Both these elements in the analysis of individual behaviour in respect of boundaries have been neglected, and their research requires different skills and aptitudes. Understanding of government boundary regulations is less demanding than investigations into the subjective environment of border-dwellers, but both approaches are complementary in understanding the relationships between boundaries and individual behaviour.

4 Electoral geography

Electoral geographers deal with two main topics. Firstly, they examine from their particular viewpoint, the voting returns of elections and plebiscites. Traditionally this has been the most important part of electoral geography. Attention is focused on the views expressed by electors about candidates and the policies they represent in elections and on matters of public importance in plebiscites. Secondly a smaller number of geographers have concentrated on the votes cast by members of parliaments, councils and other administrative bodies. The rationale for this investigation is that representatives should vote on issues in accordance with the best interests of the people whom they represent. Some issues will have a strong regional impact, and such matters are the prime concern of electoral geographers dealing with this second main aspect. These two aspects require different techniques and lead to distinct conclusions, so they are most conveniently considered separately.

The geographical study of elections and plebiscites

The responsibility of the political geographer is to describe the pattern of votes cast in elections and plebiscites, and to explain, as far as he is able, why that particular pattern developed. Description must precede explanation, and there are two main features to be described. Elections and plebiscites are always conducted according to certain rules, and these rules may largely explain the pattern of votes. Therefore the rules must be clearly understood, and the geographical characteristics of the electoral system must be described first. After this it is possible to move on to describe the pattern of votes cast.

One of the most important reasons for thoroughly understanding the electoral system is that it may be so biased as to make any further examination of the votes pointless. For example, where voters can only vote for one candidate, as in most communist states and several one-party states in Africa, the pattern of votes will not help geographical research. Theoretically it would be interesting to examine the incidence of abstentions by electors, but in one-party states such figures are not usually reported with accuracy. The system would also defy useful analysis if there was a very limited franchise as in the case of the Rhodesian electorate of the early sixties. The irregular application of rules in countries would make geographical analysis of the results fruitless. In some African elections nomination of opposition candidates has been prevented; polling booths have been placed in such a manner that opposition voters have difficulty in voting; ballot boxes have not been provided in areas of opposition strength; and if all else failed the results have been falsified. The value of a plebiscite can be reduced if the choice of responses is unnaturally restricted. For example, when the people of the Cameroons under British Trusteeship were invited to determine their future by the United Nations, they had a choice of selecting union with Nigeria or with Cameroun. There was no possibility of voting for independence from both states, although some chiefs to whom I spoke at the time, would have preferred this course. The persons who may vote in a plebiscite may also be restricted to ensure a particular result. This occurred in the 1964 referendum in Uganda to determine the future of two counties – Buyaga and Bugangazzi. Only persons who had been eligible to vote in the 1962 elections were permitted to take part in the referendum; this excluded 20,000 ex-servicemen who had moved into the area from Buganda since 1962. These people would probably have voted strongly for continued union with Buganda; instead a majority of 8,000 transferred the counties to Bunyoro.

In an earlier paper (Prescott 1959a, 301) it was suggested that gerrymandered electoral boundaries might invalidate the interpretation of election statistics. This suggestion is wrong; gerrymandering will invalidate any interpretation of the final result in terms of seats won by various parties, but it will still be worthwhile, providing the election was fair in other respects, to examine the pattern of voting by individuals. Geographers in the past have made a useful contribution to the study of gerrymandering, and recently there have been three useful additions in this field. Taylor (1971) is preparing a comprehensive bibliography of 'political redistricting', which promises to be most helpful to those geographers studying gerrymandering, when the final draft is prepared. Orr (1969) prepared an excellent paper exposing persistent gerrymandering in congressional redistributions in North Carolina. Glanville (1970) examined 'spatial biases' in electoral distributions, with particular reference to the 1955 redistribution of federal seats in the Australian state of Victoria. He distinguishes between two types of spatial bias. The first is the familiar gerrymander. This is a technique of drawing electoral boundaries so that one party wastes very few votes while other parties waste large numbers of votes. This can be done in three ways. Firstly opposition votes can be wasted by designing electorates where they poll not more than 49% of the vote.

In such cases opposition strongholds are divided and the fragments swallowed by adjoining areas dominated by the party organizing the gerrymander. In the ideal operation of this technique one party would win all the seats with 51% of the votes. The second way in which opposition votes can be wasted is by enclosing them in as few electorates as possible. These electorates are won with massive majorities, while the other party wins more seats with narrow majorities. The ideal operation of this system would leave the opposition with one or two seats, where they polled 99% of the vote, while the other party won many more seats with majorities of 51%. The final type of gerrymander occurs when scattered centres of party support are gathered together within curiously shaped electorates so that this seat can be won. Pounds (1963, 215) provides some good examples of such electorates.

There are two ways in which tests can be made to discover whether any gerrymander has possibly occurred. First, the map of constituencies can be inspected to discover whether there are any convoluted electorates, which may have been drawn to include scattered areas of support. Such an investigation is helped if the map showing the boundaries also includes information about physical features, roads and railways and settlements. Second, the wastage of votes can be shown on a graph which records the percentage of votes gained by any party for every seat contested. The seats are arranged in declining order of percentages. Fig.4.1 shows two graphs; the first graph shows a situation where neither side is favoured; the second reveals that gerrymandering has favoured Party B at the expense of Party A. If the wastage of votes does appear to put one party at a disadvantage, the detailed returns for electoral subdivisions can then be scrutinized, to see how this has been managed. One word of warning must be given to political geographers investigating the possibility of gerrymandering. It is perfectly possible that an apparent gerrymander will occur even with the honest application of sound principles. Voters for different parties are distributed unequally throughout the state, and if a regular pattern of electorates was drawn one party might be favoured. If an irregular pattern based on community of interest is drawn, the wastage of votes by one party is still possible. For example, in federal elections in Victoria from 1955 to 1966 the Country Party, which represents farming interests, polled 7–8% of the vote, while the Democratic Labor Party attracted 12–15%, yet the Country Party regularly won five seats while the Democratic Labor Party was never successful. This anomaly is explained by the fact that the strength of the Democratic Labor Party is evenly distributed throughout the State whereas the Country Party vote is strongly concentrated in rural areas.

The second kind of bias is caused by having wide variations in the enrolment in different electorates. In such cases seats with fewer voters will be easier to win than seats with large numbers of voters. Each vote in this case is not equal. An equal distribution of voters among electorates is impossible to achieve in practice, but it is possible to avoid serious weighting. However, in some cases weighting is a deliberate policy for perfectly correct reasons. In Australia and South Africa

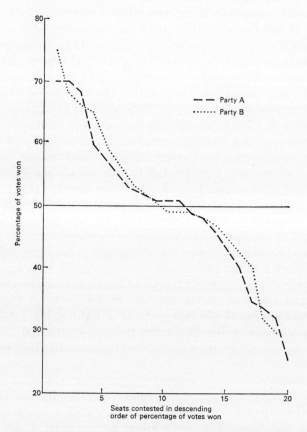

4.1b *A pattern of voting consistent with a fair distribution of electorates.*

rural electorates are favoured by having fewer voters. This is in response to the argument that if they had the same enrolments as urban electorates, they would be too large to be properly represented by a single member. As it is the West Australian electorate of Kalgoorlie has an area of 897,815 square miles! There are two ways in which weighting can be measured. Firstly, the actual distribution of voters can be compared with the perfect distribution and the mean deviation calculated. The distribution with the lowest deviation will be the least weighted.

Second, it is possible to calculate the Dauer–Kelsay Index of Representativeness (Dauer and Kelsay 1955). This index is defined as 'the smallest percentage of a state's population which could theoretically elect a majority of the lower house' (*ibid.*, 571). In fact that definition

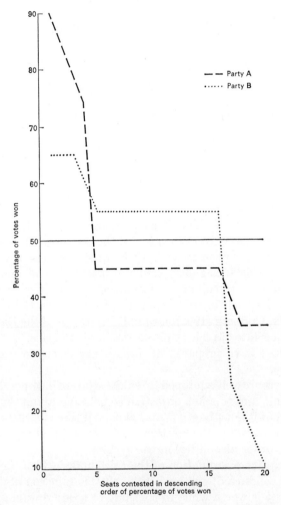

4.1a *A pattern of voting which suggests electoral malpractice.*

is not accurate, since the index relates to the *total* population of the smallest electorates which will give a majority of members. The index is calculated in the following way. The single member electorates are arranged in ascending order of numbers of voters; then starting with the smallest electorate, the votes in successive electorates are totalled until a majority of the electorates is achieved. The following example shows how the calculation is done:

Electorate	Enrolment
A	1,324
B	1,569
C	1,870
D	1,990
E	2,568
F	3,025
G	3,980
	16,326

Total of electorates A, B, C, and D = 6,753 voters
Total A, B, C, D, as percentage of total enrolment = 41·3%
Index of Representativeness = 41·3

This index can only be used to compare distributions for legislatures with equal numbers of seats. For example, the index for a parliament of 25 seats, which each contained 4% of the electorate would be 52. The index for a parliament of 20 seats with equal numbers of voters would be 55. Kaiser (1968) has suggested the calculation of another index, which can be used to compare distributions with different numbers of seats, but it is much more complicated to calculate than the Dauer–Kelsay index. Godberg (1962) has published tables of the Dauer–Kelsay index for the States in The United States of America, and Alker and Russett (1964) have prepared an interesting discussion on measures of inequality.

Geographers are well-equipped to make a study of both gerrymandering and weighting, and to reach objective conclusions about their existence or absence; but it must be stressed that even if these features are present together or separately, the election statistics will still repay analysis if there are no other disabilities in the system.

The descriptive examination of the rules under which the election or plebiscite is conducted, will serve the valuable function of demonstrating whether it is worth while to continue to a description and analysis of voting. If the franchise is heavily qualified, or if the polling arrangments are unfair, there will be little point in studying the predictable results. A recent survey (Prescott 1970) showed that there were seventy-one countries where the results were theoretically suitable for geographical examination, while in fifty-seven countries the electoral system made such analysis fruitless.

If the system is worth geographical analysis the first task is to describe the voting patterns which occur. Fortunately this is not difficult

for election statistics provide precise totals of votes for various candidates, or issues in a plebiscite, which were cast in precise areas. Two
general rules should always apply. Firstly, the voting statistics should be
plotted for the smallest possible areas. In South Africa and the United
Kingdom the constituency is the smallest division in national elections;
votes collected from all polling booths in any constituency are mixed
together in a central tally room before counting begins. In Australia
the statistics are published by polling booths, although voters in the
constituency may vote at any polling booth. However, if one assumes
that the great majority of people will vote at the nearest polling booth
a very accurate picture of the distribution of votes can be gained.
The smaller the division used the more detailed and accurate will be
the final pattern of voting. Secondly, because of the large differences in
area between rural and urban constituencies, choropleth shading should
be avoided. Proportional symbols related to the number of voters are
most satisfactory (Prescott 1959a). The recent atlas of voting in the
United Kingdom by Kinnear (1968) is a very bad example of mapping
electoral distributions. He shows election results for Britain since 1885
by a series of choropleth maps, including several insets, which all lack
a linear scale.

Individual geographers will find different facets of the voting returns
to describe, but it is recommended that at least the following three
features are always considered. First the electoral boundaries should be
described, preferably in clear maps with reference to the official descriptions. Changes in electoral boundaries should also be described,
and maps to show the persistence of certain electoral boundaries can
easily be constructed (Stanley 1968). The second and major aspect is
to describe the pattern of voting, and this can only be undertaken
after the voting system has been understood. Methods of voting form a
very complex subject; fortunately, since there are many excellent books
on this material, it is unnecessary to describe them here (Lakeman 1970;
Mackenzie 1958; and Van den Burgh 1955). It is important to stress
that different systems will require different treatment during the preparation of maps and diagrams. For example, in the first-past-the-post
system used in England, where the candidate with the most votes is
elected to represent single-member constituencies, it is important to
distinguish seats where the victor won more than half the votes from
those where he won less than the combined total of his opponents.
Again, in the alternative vote system used in many elections in Australia, if the final figures are used after any necessary distribution of
preferences, the votes for minor parties will have disappeared. The
selection of which figures to use will sometimes require political judge-
ments, especially in discarding tiny votes for independents or splinter
parties, or amalgamating votes from two candidates, perhaps one

official and one unofficial, who really represent the same party platform.

Once these decisions have been made the voting statistics can be shown in a variety of standard ways. Frequently the percentage of votes obtained by different parties in the various constituencies is plotted (Prescott 1959b). In other cases the total votes cast in the election for a single party is calculated, and the proportion contributed by each constituency is then computed and plotted. This is useful in identifying areas of party strengths and weaknesses. Lewis and Skipworth (1966) used the total number of votes cast for a party to identify the average vote for each constituency; then they plotted the actual constituency vote as a deviation from this average.

In addition to identifying the distribution of votes cast, it is useful to measure the varying turnout of voters in different areas. This also indicates the rate of abstention throughout the constituencies. Providing that the abstentions are recorded accurately, these figures will be useful in detecting areas of opposition when the choice of candidates in an election or alternatives in a plebiscite is limited, as in one-party states.

The plotting on maps of such distributions for individual elections is a useful technique in identifying the trends in voting over a long period. Trends can be observed by comparing several maps of successive elections but it is preferable to record the trend in one or two maps. If the electoral boundaries are only changed after long intervals, trend maps can be prepared very easily for the intervals. The vote obtained by a particular party in each division at various elections can be represented on a graph, in the way that rainfall distributions are often shown. It is also possible to classify the seats in terms of results into categories such as 'safe Conservative', 'marginal Labour', and 'swinging' to give some identification of their electoral history. Such classifications should be based on some carefully designed objective system when there are several seats to be considered. In some countries, however, there are frequent changes in electoral boundaries, and this poses a real problem if trend maps are required. Stanley (1968) faced this problem in producing trend maps of elections in New South Wales between 1932 and 1965, and solved it in a very sensible and useful way. In Australia votes are recorded by subdivisions of electorates. These subdivisions have a greater persistence than the electorates which they form and Stanley constructed his maps around these units. At various redistributions subdivisions are amalgamated in different ways to form electorates; sometimes the subdivisions are divided, but frequently they are transferred as a whole from one electorate to another. Stanley established that 606 subdivisions had existed during the time he considered. Fifty-nine of these were discarded, either because they had existed for only two elections, or because their boundaries had been drastically altered. The remainder were either unaltered during their lifetime, or were not appreciably altered. The percentage of Labor and non-Labor vote was calculated for each election in each subdivision. The subdivisions were then classified by the proportion of elections they had returned Labor or non-Labor candidates. For example, those subdivisions which had given one party a simple majority in at least 75% of elections, were described as *consistent* Labor or non-Labor areas. It was also possible to show when there had been a change in allegiance within the period, or if the seat showed no consistent pattern. The information was recorded in symbols of uniform size located at the geographic centre of the subdivision. The resulting maps provided a very interesting picture of trends and certainly identified those areas which were worth further detailed study, either as samples of regions which provided uniform support, or regions where party preferences fluctuated.

In seeking to provide a geographical explanation of the electoral system the political geographer should focus on two main aspects. The first aspect concerns the electoral system used, and the way it is applied. Explanations will usually be found in the structure of the population and the motives of the government selecting the system. Some governments wish to prevent the development of splinter parties or the representation of minorities, and so they avoid proportional representation or the semi-proportional systems such as the limited vote and the cumulative vote. Other governments, by contrast, wish to allow minorities to be represented and so use the proportional systems or weight electorates in favour of concentrated minorities. Some governments anxious to remain in power construct franchise regulations which disbar sections of the electorate from participation. The struggle to register Negro voters in some southern States is a recent memory, and the present electoral system in Rhodesia is certainly designed to retain political control for Europeans for as long as possible. Other governments may cling to power through the use of gerrymandering or weighting.

The second aspect deals with the division of the country into electorates where this is required by the system. In some countries electorates are drawn by independent commissioners, in others by the government in power. While redistributions are regular features in some countries, such as Australia, in other states redistributions are irregular, and marked imbalances can develop in the numbers of electors in various seats, due to internal migration. The principles on which redistributions are based are frequently made public, and generally they are principles which the geographer is well qualified to test. For example, in the 1968 federal redistribution in Victoria, Australia, the Commissioners were given the following instructions. Thirty-four divisions had to be created of which none was to contain more than 62,009 voters or less than 41,340 voters. Boundaries were to be drawn with regard to community of economic, social and regional interests; means of communication within the division with special reference to disabilities arising out of remoteness; the trend of population within the State; the density of population within the division; the area of the division; the physical features of the division; and the existing boundaries of divisions and subdivisions (Commonwealth of Australia 1968, 9–10). The eventual distribution can be investigated in terms of these principles, and the extent to which future trends were accurately estimated can be assessed as new population figures become available. Explanation of the electoral system and such boundaries as are necessary, has not formed an important part of electoral geography, a fact demonstrated by the useful bibliography prepared by Goodey (1968), but it is as much part of the subject as the explanation of voting patterns, which has received much more attention.

Traditionally electoral geographers, such as Siegfried, Krebheil, Wright, Goguel, Hugonnier and Burghardt explained voting patterns according to a simple plan. They made the basic assumption that people will vote according to what they perceive to be their best interests. They then explored the characteristics of voters which might give a clue to the nature of their self-interest. The areal variations in social and economic class, religion, nationality and race were among the prime factors considered. Using such methods political geographers seemed to explain the foundations of voting patterns, for whole countries or large sections, and be able to predict how patterns would change as the franchise altered, or as migration occurred. Pelling (1967) has tried to distinguish between the ecological approach, which relates political behaviour to the voter's environment and his pattern of social life, and the sociological approach, which explores the relationships between political behaviour and the voter's social class, occupation and ethnic origin. He suggests that the ecological and sociological approaches will be best in rural and urban environments respectively. This division will not be acceptable to most geographers and Pelling's excellent book does not in fact support this dichotomy.

This traditional approach is now under attack by a new school of electoral geographers represented by Cox, Archer, Reynolds and Brown. They consider the traditional approach to have two main defects. Firstly, the correlation of aggregate data such as votes and economic status does not allow any difference or prediction to be made about individual behaviour (Cox 1968, 58; Cox 1969, 109; and Reynolds and Archer 1969, 2). Secondly, it is argued that since the traditional approach is used by political scientists, it is not distinctively geographical. These defects lead these geographers to recommend an approach which focuses on spatial processes such as contagion, and contextual influences (Cox 1968; Cox 1969, 112–3; and Reynolds and Archer 1969, 31). The justification for these contemporary proposals cannot be found in the alleged shortcomings of traditional studies. Geographers have not wished to make inferences about individual behaviour, they have been much more concerned with aggregate behaviour in discrete regions. It is important for an electoral geographer to be able to show that in the mining valleys of South Wales most of the electors will vote for the Labour Party; that in Northern Ireland the main Catholic areas give strongest support to non-Unionist parties; and that in much of West Africa party strength relates closely to tribal distributions. The interest of political scientists in correlations of aggregate statistics is not sufficient cause for geographers to abandon this approach in favour of something more distinctive. There is every reason why political geographers and political scientists should share common ground; it has already been suggested that the lack of interest in political geography by political scientists has been to the disadvantage of the subject. Studies in electoral geography by political scientists, such as Rantala (1967), are certain to help concepts in the field. In any case political scientists, such as Foladare (1968), are already considering some of the spatial processes which Cox and others regard as being specifically geographic.

The justification for the new spatial approach must therefore be sought in its own strength rather than the weakness of established procedures. Unfortunately all the advocates of the new approach are very tentative in their conclusions and a final assessment of their work must await further evidence. Despite this fact, it is still necessary to make some comments on the material already published. Reynolds and Archer (1969) set out to ascertain whether areal variations of socio-economic characteristics provide a satisfactory explanation of patterns of party support. This is attempted through a complicated mathematical analysis of data relating to votes cast in the 1967 Mayoral election in Indianapolis and censal data for 1960.

> First, the areal distribution of the vote for the selected election is tested for correspondence with a normal distribution. Second, this distribution is examined in its spatial array for a significant deviation from randomness. Third, a principal components analysis of the set of explanatory variables selected is undertaken. Fourth, after presenting the results of the principal components analysis, the components scores are tested both for normality and contiguity. Fifth, the proportion of the voters within the areal units who supported one party is regressed against the results of the previous analysis. Sixth, residuals from this regression are tested for normality and for remaining contiguity. (Reynolds and Archer 1969, 21)

Since the boundaries of precincts, within which votes were cast, did not match the censal tracts, votes were assumed to be uniform throughout the precincts and distributed to the tracts accordingly. At the end of the mathematical process 82% of the variation in the distribution of votes had been explained by selected explanatory variables, of which easily the most important were socio-economic class and race. The contiguity ratio, which measures similarity of voting in adjacent divisions, was 13·99; which enables the authors to say that 'spatial contagion between areal units at the census tract level was an operative factor in determining the spatial result of the Indianapolis mayoral election of 1967' (Reynolds and Archer 1969, 29). However, when the contiguity factor was calculated at the precinct level, the contiguity ratio rose to 26·44. The dilemma is that it cannot be established whether this greater propensity for adjoining precincts to vote in similar ways is due to shorter communication distances, or the increasing socio-economic homogeneity of precincts. In short, it is to be expected that the contiguity ratio will increase as the size of the units being considered is reduced, since in many areas the contiguous area of party support will be larger than the electoral subdivisions. Further, presumably different contiguity ratios would be created by different patterns of boundaries.

Since Cox (1969, 112) admits that much of his paper dealing with the influence of the spatial context on voting decisions is speculative, it is not proposed to consider it at length here, but two comments must be made. The first concerns a point which he stresses, that changes in the pattern of voting over any period will be due to relocation of the voters by migration and variations in the information flowing through any network to individual voters (Cox 1969, 87 and 101). This view neglects the importance of the physical replacement of the electorate through the continuous process of births and deaths, which Butler and Stokes (1969, 4) stress very strongly, and the possibilities of changes in franchise qualifications. Further, it is essential to the argument that Cox should demonstrate that the flow of information can be measured and that its influence on voters can be assessed. This is an extremely complex matter. For example, different age groups generally have differing degrees of susceptibility to political information; indeed this is so pronounced that Butler and Stokes (1969, 44–64) can distinguish a political life cycle for most individuals. This point is also confirmed by Glenn and Grimes (1968). Further, studies by scholars outside geography have shown that it is persons who are less exposed to information who are most likely to change their views (Butler and Stokes 1969, 221).

If geographers follow the advice of Reynolds and Archer and Cox and concentrate on these spatial processes, they will be abandoning a road of proven reliability for a track which may lead into regions of sociology where they are ill-equipped to survive. It will need many more studies of larger areas than a suburb or a city, over a number of elections, to signpost the way, before the analysis of spatial processes becomes a major part of electoral geography. For example, the problem of interpreting some of the answers given by sample populations has not received sufficient attention from supporters of the new trends. Even if it is accepted that the answers are given after careful and honest consideration, and that will not always be the case, there is still the problem of interpreting similar answers which may mask important variations. For example, there is a high risk in assuming that religion, as a factor, is equally important to all respondents who claim membership of a particular faith, or that all people who completed secondary education can be treated as a single group. My own experience in talking to individuals about the way they voted in particular elections, is that many do not know exactly why they voted as they did. Certainly in rationalizing their decision no one has ever explained their vote in terms of the flow of information or the political complexion of the area in which they live.

The discussion by Reynolds and Archer, which leads to the gloomy and unnecessary conclusion that if economic and class characteristics provide sufficient explanation of voting patterns the field should be left to political scientists, contains a clue to one aspect of spatial process which political geographers might consider. I refer to the processes which create socio-economic or ethnic regions within a city or a country. Much work has already been done by urban and population geographers in this field, and such processes would be much more credible and easier to measure than processes involving the transmission of information across a bewildering series of formal and informal networks.

Until the value of the new techniques discussed above has been proved, the following stages are recommended to electoral geographers searching for explanations of voting patterns.

The description of voting patterns referred to earlier in this chapter will complete the first stage, which is the identification of areas of party preponderance in the most detailed fashion possible. These patterns should be established for individual elections and for periods covering several votes. Different criteria for establishing areas of party preponderance will be used by geographers dealing with different countries, but they should be clearly stated, and will generally include a minimum level of support for a specified period. In identifying the areas of greatest party strength, those intervening areas where no party dominates will also be discovered. The second stage should focus on areas of party preponderance such as the coalfields of England, the English-speaking areas of Natal, Negro ghettoes in some American cities and tribal areas in West Africa. If the reasonable assumption is made, that individuals vote in accordance with what they perceive to be their best interests, the first search must be for population characteristics which appear to distinguish groups of common interest. Such characteristics would include race, perceived social and economic status, nationality and age. The degree of coincidence between patterns of votes and the distribution of population characteristics can be established by recognized mathematical techniques, such as those used by Roberts and Rumage (1965) and McPhail (1970), or cartographic methods such as that devised by Lewis (1965) which is described in chapter 2. Whichever method is used, any transformation of data which is necessary should be carefully described, so that other workers do not have to take the results on trust. In many cases there will be a marked correspondence between votes and population characteristics. While it is true, as Cox stresses, that even a high correlation will not permit inferences about the behaviour of a specific individual, this will not worry many electoral geographers, who are probably more concerned with voters in groups. If there is a low correlation between votes in an area where one party dominates and the characteristics of the voters living there, further investigation will be necessary. The discrepancy will generally have two types of characteristics. The first deals with the homogeneity or heterogeneity of the characteristics of the voters. In some situations, an area occupied by a uniform population will give massive support for some unexpected party. In other cases a region populated by a heterogeneous population will cast almost all its votes for a single party. Secondly, discrepancies may also be long-term or short-term. The short-term discrepancies might only exist for one election, and these are often easy to explain. The answer will usually be found in local issues, if the discrepancy is confined to one area, and in national issues if there are widespread anomalies. For example, when Mr Goldwater contested the American presidency there was a widespread defection of Republican voters in former Republican strongholds, and a widespread defection of Democratic voters from some southern strongholds of that party. This was clearly a national issue, and subsequent presidential elections showed that it was a short-term discrepancy. If over a long period a region with a heterogeneous population structure lends overwhelming support to one party, the answer will often be found in the personality of the sitting member. The discrepancy often ends with the retirement of a popular local candidate after a long career. If the explanation seems to be cast in terms of the personality of candidates or issues which lack any geographical component, such as abolition of the death penalty, or the introduction of abortion on request, it seems unlikely that the electoral geographer can pursue the matter, and such explanations in detail can be left to the sociologist, the political scientist and the social historian.

It should also be remembered that certain features of the electoral system may promote certain anomalies. For example, in safe seats for one party it is possible for its supporters to register a protest vote without damaging the party; this luxury is scarcely available for people living in a marginal constituency. Further, the system of preferential voting, as in Australia, allows a vote to be cast in the first instance for some unimportant candidate, in the safe knowledge that such a candidate will be eliminated and the second or third preference will return to the preferred party.

The electoral geographer, after dealing with areas of party preponderance, can then turn his attention to the other areas where no party enjoys pre-eminence. In this case if the voting population posseses a diversity of significant characteristics the explanation may be simple. Party strengths may be equivalent because there is a balance of voters supporting each party. The discrepancy in this case will concern a region which is occupied by a homogeneous group of voters in terms of their social and economic features. It is then necessary to explain how such a uniform population divides its loyalties between competing parties. The task of explanation will be easier when two of the parties competing have similar policies. This would be the situation where a splinter party, not significantly different from its parent, emerged or when an independent party candidate stood in opposition to the official party candidate. The explanation will often be found in political personalities and local issues which cut across party lines. Protest votes against an incumbent government in safe seats, in by-elections, and under systems of alternative votes may also help to explain anomalies in these situations. The level of turn-out will often be related to the marginal nature of the seat. Turn-out is often higher in marginal seats than in safe seats (Hampton 1968).

In addition to explaining the stability of areas of party preponderence and areas evenly contested, the electoral geographer must also explain why these patterns change either for a short term, which has already been mentioned, or over a long period. Many explanations of long-term changes will be found. The physical replacement of the electorate as voters die and young people qualify for the vote will be a powerful explanation of very long-term changes. The introduction of new voters through immigration from overseas, or changes in the franchise qualifications, may also be very significant. The success of the Australian Labor Party in Western Australian State elections in February 1971, owed something to the fact that the people added to the lists by lowering the voting age to 18 years favoured the Labor Party. The internal migration of voters will also account for some changes in electoral patterns. Cox (1968) has discussed some of the significant features of the movement from central urban areas to peri-urban districts, which is so common in many cities. Issues will also be important in explaining new alignments of party support. Some issues will only create transitory changes, but others, such as Home Rule for Ireland, will produce new and lasting cleavages.

The extent to which this programme can be successfully pursued will depend on the areal units for which voting statistics are available, and the extent to which information about population characteristics is available, either in identical units, or units which can be manipulated, for the approximate time the election was held. If the electoral units are very large the electoral regions which can be distinguished will be coarse, and the correlations which can be obtained may be unsatis-factory; students in Australia are fortunate because very detailed election results are published, which make it possible to produce very detailed maps of electoral regions. If there is a long interval between the taking of a census and the casting of votes there are obvious dangers in relying too heavily on any correlations obtained, especially in peri-urban areas where population growth is most rapid through migration.

The geographical study of votes in international and national assemblies

This branch of the subject has received very little attention from elec-toral geographers, since the votes of American Congressmen on major issues were recorded on maps in 1932 (Paullin 1932). More recently the subject has been explored in some detail by political scientists, such as Russett (1966) and Friedheim (1967). Any investigation of votes cast in assemblies has one or two aims. Some studies use votes cast by na-tional or regional representatives to classify those countries or regions into groups. This has been the major aim of both Russett and Fried-heim. To this aim could also be added the desire to interpret the vote in order to decipher the attitude of the country or electorate represented.

These are both legitimate aims for political geographers, but there are a number of reasons why they have not attracted more attention. Firstly, there is little point in classifying states by votes in international assemblies, or any other way, unless the classification is going to be used as a starting point for analysis. Political geographers, such as Fisher, East and Spate, who have written some of the very best regional political geography, were dealing with obvious regions, such as Indo-China, or the Mediterranean, which do not require involved calculations before they can be clearly discerned. Further, most geographers will be concerned that voting alignments may not be sufficiently permanent to justify using them for the preparation of textbooks or courses of lectures. Lastly, the use of different combinations of votes would furnish different groupings. In short, there are simpler means of distin-guishing regions in political geography than by the analysis of votes in the United Nations. Second, many geographers are concerned that votes in assemblies may not always be very significant in terms of the country or electorate represented. For example, in the United Nations many votes are cast for issues in the certain knowledge that no action will be taken if the resolution is carried. In addition many votes are taken on resolutions with many points; some states, while in broad agreement with most of the resolution, will still vote against it if one section contains something which is unacceptable. It is also possible that the form of the resolution may not accurately reflect the opinion of the government concerned, in the same way that referenda do not always allow a full choice of alternatives. Considering votes in national parliaments, it is apparent that in many cases regional interests are submerged by the party line on a particular issue. In any case there is no guarantee that the elected representative is reflecting the views of even a simple majority of his electors. The machinery by which members consult with their constituents is not very efficient and is rarely very sensitive. In any case the study of votes cast in national and international assemblies in order to interpret the attitudes of the governments or electors represented, can never provide a substitute for the analysis of speeches made during the debate, where finer shades of meaning can be conveyed than by a vote in favour or against.

If this aspect of electoral geography is to be further developed it will probably be along the following lines. Firstly, geographers will use the statistical analysis of votes about matters which have a definite geographical significance at international assemblies and conferences in order to identify groups of countries which have similar attitudes. Friedheim's study of the United Nations conferences on the law of the sea is an excellent example of this kind of study. Votes in meetings of the General Agreement on Tariffs and Trade might also be profitably considered. Votes on questions such as disarmament and the structure of the United Nations seems to have little geographical significance and these subjects may be left to the consideration of political scientists and historians. Once the groups with a common attitude have been identified the electoral geographer can then explore the extent to which the groups also share common motives.

Secondly, geographers may be interested in considering the votes of delegates to constitutional conferences during the evolution of the state in order to find out the extent of differences in regional attitudes. This would be particularly useful when the question of a federal or unitary constitution was being considered. Such studies could include historical cases, typified by the excellent study of the secessionist conventions in the southern United States by Wooster (1962).

5 Political geography and public policy

A growing concern with the policies of international organizations, national governments and local authorities has been a recent trend in political geography, which has matched the tendency for economic geographers to study the policies of individual firms and groups of companies. This development can be traced to the realization that the policies of administrations and commercial organizations are powerful forces in shaping changes in the cultural and physical landscape, and alterations in existing patterns of exchange and the distributions of people and economic activities. These policies of political authorities may be more important in influencing patterns of economic development than the physical features of climate, topography and resources.

The term 'public policy' in the title of this chapter has two meanings. Firstly, it refers to policies determined by governments or government agencies, including international and sub-national authorities to which some powers have been delegated by national governments. It does not refer to the policies of commercial firms, although the policies of some giant firms, such as oil companies, will be of interest to political geographers studying the Middle East. The governments in this case can either be *de jure* or *de facto*. The policies of the *de facto* government of Biafra were largely responsible for developments within that area during the period from May 1967 until January 1970. For long periods of the war in Vietnam, the policies of the Viet Cong have been more significant to certain parts of South Vietnam than the policies of the government of Saigon. Finally, the lack of recognition for the Rhodesian Government after the seizure of independence in November 1965 has not hindered the application of its domestic policies. Political geographers will also find it useful to include in the category of public policy those policies advocated by organizations which seek political power or changes in the state's social, political and economic structure through political action. These groups would include political parties outside the government, regional and sectional pressure groups, and ethnic and other associations seeking administrative changes or supporting secessionist movements. The studies by McColl (1967 and

1969) dealing with internal revolution, and the study of new state movements by geographers such as Woolmington (1966) are examples of these kinds of study.

'Public policy' also refers to those policies which are known to exist because it is impossible to consider policies which are secret. This obvious point is made to draw attention to the need to recognize that certain policies, particularly those relating to defence, and sometimes those relating to territorial arrangements, are not made public at the time of their formation. The analysis of such policies will be made only after their existence has been discovered through the opening of archives, or disclosures following changes of government or changes in political personalities.

There are three main aspects of any exploration of public policy as part of political geography. Firstly, it is essential to identify the types of policy which should be considered, and the classification of such policies which will best serve comparative studies in political geography. Secondly, it is necessary to understand the relationships which exist between political geography and public policy. Thirdly the methods of analysis and the problems associated with them must be investigated.

The scope and classification of public policies suitable for study by political geographers

It is no longer fashionable to question the value of a particular contribution to the subject by asking 'But is it geography?' This was a familiar phrase to academics in England in the years following the Second World War; it had the disadvantage of restricting the field, but the advantage that any work done was clearly in the best traditions of the subject. In more recent years the bounds of geography have been pushed wider and wider and this trend has had two main consequences. Firstly, many geographers today are closer to workers in neighbouring fields than they are to other geographers. This statement does not refer only to the divisions between physical and human geography, but to the more dangerous divisions between physical geographers and between human geographers. Secondly, the expansion of the field has meant that certain areas of the subject, which have yielded rich harvests in the past, are now being neglected. One such area is regional geography, which is becoming of increasing interest to historians and economists. Instead of profiting from this interdisciplinary interest, more and more geographers are using it as an excuse for increasing systematic specialization.

It is because of these dangers, and because I have played some part in advancing the study of policy by geographers (Prescott 1968), that it seems worth while to specify as exactly as possible which policies should receive most attention from political geographers.

There are three tests which political geographers can apply to discover whether study of the policy would be worth while. A positive answer to any of them is sufficient. The first test examines whether the application of the policy has any direct influence on the physical or cultural landscape. Geographers must be aware of the significance of migration policies which influence the distribution and movement of people; of zoning policies which restrict the range of land-use in different areas; of farm-support and tariff policies which encourage the establishment and survival of specific industries; and of transport policies which influence the location of activities and the movements of goods and people. There is no suggestion that only political geographers will be interested in such policies, but it is the policies of governments and government agencies which form the most important facet of the areal differentiation of political units. This test will identify the majority of policies in which political geographers have an interest.

The second test discovers whether the application of the policy is influenced by the operation of geographical factors. No exhaustive list of geographical factors can be given, but some examples will show the possible range. Climatic variations may influence the success of farm-support programmes and the extension of irrigated areas. Distinctive population characteristics may create a measure of regional nationalism which will wreck policies connected with local administration and parliamentary representation This certainly happened in Northern Ireland and East Pakistan during 1971. Severe variation in levels of production throughout the world can adversely affect the operation of international price agreements for various commodities.

The final test distinguishes those policies which were formed in the light of geographical factors. This simply means that the decision-makers took certain geographical factors into account: it does not imply that geographical factors were decisive in the final policy decisions. For example, decisions about principles to govern the division of a state into constituencies are made after the careful study of population distributions and the ease of communication in various areas. Policies relating to regional development should be based on a thorough knowledge of the distribution of resources and present levels of economic development. Policies to destroy secessionist movements are made after assessments of the importance of the area concerned in economic and strategic terms, and the influence which such policies may have on other areas of the state.

Clearly many policies will satisfy all three tests, which have been placed in this specific order because of the ease with which the tests can be answered. It is generally easier to identify the geographical result of policies than to discover whether decision-makers took geographical factors into account. In fact the three tests have been included on grounds of theoretical completeness, for I am unable to think of a policy where geographical factors influenced its formulation and where no geographical consequences followed from its operation. What is certain is that if the policy satisfies none of these tests, it is not appropriate for consideration by political geographers. Thus recent Australian policies relating to the maintenance of law and order, the collection of fines from trades unions, and the penalties incurred by teachers who strike, are of no professional interest to political geographers.

Having identified the policies which should be considered it is now necessary to discuss how they should be classified to simplify comparative studies in the field.

It is perhaps necessary to stress that the classification should be based on the qualities of the policy rather than on the qualities of the government. For example, it was once suggested in a seminar which I attended, that the comparison of government policies should be based on the qualities of government *structure*, government *process* and the *stage* of economic and political development. But exploration of this proposal revealed many difficulties. In terms of government structure, it would be very difficult to distinguish all the important groups. It is tempting to nominate only unitary and federal states, but these categories stand at opposite ends of a spectrum, which contains a bewildering variety of quasi-federal systems. Government process presumably refers to democratic or authoritarian systems, but again it is hard to draw a clear line which separates them. Thus it would be difficult for geographers to agree in defining any government in terms of structure and process. But perhaps a more important criticism is that diverse governments will use identical policies, even though they will not always have identical motives. The difficulty of classifying governments, however, is slight compared with problems of defining states in terms of their economic and political development.

The problem of classifying policies is complicated by the many different facets which they possess. Each policy originates at a particular level of government, at a particular time, applying to a particular subject; it may influence the total population or sections of the population, and may apply to the whole area of the state or certain parts of it; policies are enforced in different ways and receive varying degrees of support from sections of the population. Lowi (1964) has suggested that policies should be classified into three groups, regulatory, distributive and redistributive. Regulatory policies restrict available alternatives and would include quotas on types of production. Distributive policies allow the donation of material and funds such as superphosphate subsidies, to sections of the population. Redistributive policies are concerned with the aquisition of funds from one source and their disbursements to others. Presumably price equalization schemes, which require consumers in Australia to pay higher prices for butter than can be obtained abroad, so that farmers can be given a subsidy, are typical of this group. The difficulty with this system is that different geographers could classify the same policy in different groups.

Any effort to weld all the different facets into a single classification would produce a multitude of classes, many of which would probably never be employed. Each political geographer engaged in studying policies will probably prefer to devise an individual system best suited to his particular needs. What is really important, is that in published work the author should provide sufficient basic information about the policy, to allow it to be fitted into other systems by other geographers. Such basic information should include the level of government which produces the policy, its subject, the section of the population and the area of the state to which it refers, and the period during which the policy is in operation.

Many geographers will find that a simple classification by subject will be adequate for their needs, and such a system has been devised (Prescott 1968). The classification is based on the assumption that any government has two main aims: the preservation of territorial integrity and the development of the state's resources to the maximum benefit of the majority of the population. The classes can be called *defence policies* and *development policies*, and it should be noted that they are not mutually exclusive. A minority of policies may serve both aims at the same time. South Africa's search for oil deposits represents such a dual policy. It is also suggested that in addition to these main groups of policies it is useful to distinguish *administrative policies*. Such policies are concerned with the process of government. They would include the division of the state into electoral areas and local government divisions; the selection of an official language; the choice of a capital; and the division of responsibilities between central and regional governments in a federation.

Each of these three main groups can be subdivided. Defence policies seek to increase the strength of the state and weaken the power of enemies or potential enemies; it is therefore sensible to divide them into those policies designed to increase the intrinsic strength of the state, and those aimed at improving the relative strength of the state. Into the first group would fall policies designed to secure new territory, which offers additional resources or strategic advantages; policies through which internal dissidence is ended; policies for improving the use of available material and human resources; and policies which secure the support of allies. The second group would include policies which exclude enemies from useful territory; policies which increased the domestic problems of opponents; policies which deprived enemies of important supplies; and policies which disrupted dangerous alliances.

Development policies can be classified according to whether they apply to the entire state or part of the state, and whether they are devised by a single government or a number of governments. This gives four classes. Firstly there are the *specific unilateral policies*. These policies are determined by a single government and apply to a particular area, or to a special sector of the economy, or to a distinct section of the population. *General unilateral policies* are also determined by a single government, but they apply to the whole area of the state, or the entire economy, or to all the citizens. *Specific multilateral* and *general multilateral policies* are similar to the categories already described, but the decision is taken by more than one government. Administrative policies of interest to political geographers will be mainly concerned with issues of *elections, the administrative structure* and *the control of people and land*.

The relationships between geography and public policy

There are three stages during the formation and operation of policy when geography may be significant. Firstly, the decision-makers may perceive certain geographical factors which will influence the policy they select. Secondly, when the policy is applied certain unperceived geographical factors may operate and influence its outcome. Thirdly, the application of certain policies may produce some geographical results. The relationships of geography and policy are shown in fig. 5.1. It shows that

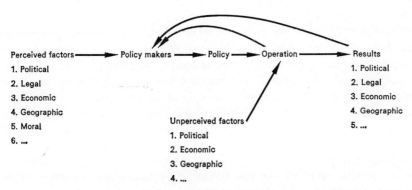

5.1 *The relationships between public policy and geography.*

experience concerning the operation and results of policies might influence the formation of new policies. It does not show that the results of one policy might lead to the development of other types of policy, although this is a common characteristic. In some cases this relationship between geography and public policy will be evident at all three stages; this would be the case in most regional development policies. In other cases although geography does not influence the formation of policy geographical consequences will flow from its application. For example, the doctrinaire decision to nationalize expatriate industries in many underdeveloped countries has had a marked influence on patterns of production, capital investment and industrial location. It seems unlikely that there will be any policies where geographical factors influence their formation, but where there are no geographical consequences following its application.

It is important to recognise that geography will be only one of many factors influencing the formation and operation of policy, and that there will be other results than geographical changes when policies are applied. Political, legal, moral and economic factors and results may also be involved, and will be studied by the appropriate specialist. The significance of this is that geographers can never hope to tell the full story of policies, their work will contribute to the complete analysis, which will also be assisted by lawyers, political scientists, economists and philosophers. It is also worth while to note that if geography is not involved in any of the three stages mentioned, then the particular policy is outside the scope of political geography.

It is now necessary to investigate the problems associated with the analysis of the relationships between geography and public policy, and the methods which may be used to solve them.

Analysis of the relationships between geography and public policy

The aim of political geographers who study policy formation is to determine the importance of geographical factors in the process. The achievement of this aim is hindered by four difficulties. Firstly, in order to understand the possible role of geographical factors it is necessary to know the process by which policy is made. This means that the geographer should know which committees and sub-committees are concerned, and in which order these committees conduct their deliberations. This is a subject which falls within the ambit of political science but in many cases there is no detailed description of the processes of policy formation, and geographers will have to acquire this information for themselves. Once the process is mastered, the second difficulty appears; this involves the identification of the decision-makers. This identification will often be easier at the level of local government, than at the level of national government. The difficulty of preparing an accurate list of the people concerned in making national economic and defence policies can be easily imagined.

Even if the decision-makers can be identified a further difficulty exists. A complete analysis of the role of geographical factors requires the study of detailed records of debate and correspondence. Too often this material is unavailable, because the records are simply brief summaries, or because they are deemed to be confidential. While it is important to know what decision was taken, it is equally important to know how the debate ranged and the different arguments which were raised before the decision was made. Readers may consider the minutes of meetings they attend, and decide whether such minutes convey an accurate impression of the reasons why decisions were taken. The discovery of detail will be easier in cases where policies are based on public commissions, where evidence is recorded in great detail and published.

The final difficulty relates to the fact that geography is only one of the factors involved; it has already been noted that political, legal, economic and moral factors will also be involved. Theoretically, an accurate assessment of the role of geographical factors could only be made in the light of perfect knowledge of the significance of all other categories of factors. Practically this is impossible for geographers to achieve, and so for this and the other reasons mentioned, geographers must realize that the final answers about the significance of geographical factors will be imperfect. However, this is not a unique situation and geographers should not be discouraged, because there are a number of methods which will help to reduce any area of uncertainty, and obviously no one is better qualified to assess the significance of geography in policy formation.

There are two recommendations which may advance the study of policy-making by political geographers. Firstly, there should be a concentration on policies where non-geographical factors are apparently at a minimum. There are many policies which may be described as being *technical*. Such policies would include decisions concerned with industrial location, the establishment of transport systems, the delinineation of administrative divisions and the extension of irrigation areas. In such cases the relevance of moral, political and legal factors is likely to be slight, and any relevance they may have will usually be obvious. Geographic factors and economic factors based in geography will often be decisive in making technical policies.

Geographers will experience more certain results by focusing on technical policies at the expense of other policies, such as the waging of war, the recognition of other states, disarmament and the application of economic socialist doctrines, where non-geographical factors will play a very important role. Secondly, there should be an emphasis on historical situations where such documentary evidence as exists is available in archives. This will reduce the amount of guesswork and the number of assumptions which would be involved in any contemporary analysis. The only contemporary subjects where corresponding detail might be available are those where decisions are taken after receiving public evidence.

The amount of material available will determine whether the analyst can use the approach of cognitive behaviourism, where the perception of individual decision-makers is reconstructed, or probabilism, where assumptions of rational behaviour are made about the decision-makers.

Before considering the problems of studying the role of geographical factors in influencing the operation of policies, it seems worth while to deal first with the geographical results of the application of policies. This transposition is necessary, since it is through the appreciation of results that the operation of unperceived factors in the second stage can be most easily identified.

The geographical results of the application of policies will be as varied as the policies themselves. For example, a decision to establish a major dam, to irrigate marginal land, will eventually alter the régime of the river below the dam, and probably change former patterns of erosion and deposition; land above the dam will be flooded, and, if the resulting lake is large enough, wave action may produce shore and cliff features; the clearing of land for cultivation will alter the patterns of natural vegetation, and the application of water to the land may change the soil characteristics; the fauna and fish in the area may be influenced by these developments. Settling farmers on the land will alter the distribution of population and lead to demands for communications and service facilities, if the population numbers are sufficient it may be necessary to create new administrative areas, and the electoral balance of the area may be changed. Production from this new area may compete with other areas in the same country and create problems of marketing. This simple illustration demonstrates that geographers with different specialist interests will find common interest in the results of policy applications. It also shows that certain policies will produce chain reactions and create the need for other policies.

There are no serious problems in establishing the geographical results of the application of various policies. Contemporary studies will naturally be unable to establish any long-term results, while the student of historical cases will often find it hard to discover some of the minor, short-term consequences of certain policies.

Four general points can be made about this particular aspect of the relationships between geography and public policy. Firstly, any geographer who embarks on this topic should be encouraged to study *all* the geographical consequences flowing from a particular policy. This suggestion is made first because so much effort will be invested in understanding the policy and its operation that it would be wasteful not to explore all the consequences. For example, it would be short-sighted for an economic geographer studying decentralization to stop short after measuring changes in industrial location. The study should be continued so that changes in population numbers and structure can be assessed, migration streams can be identified and changes in patterns of electoral support can be established. The second reason for making this suggestion is that other geographers and scholars from other disciplines will be glad to have all the geographical consequences of a single policy in one place, rather than searching for them in a wide variety of different sources.

The second point, which has been mentioned before, is simply that it is unnecessary for geographical factors to have been significant in the formation of policy for that policy to have geographical consequences; thus doctrinaire policies should not be ignored.

Thirdly, many policies are designed to prevent change, to preserve the *status quo* in respect of levels of production or volumes of trade. In this case the influence of the policy will only be identified by considering the trends which existed before the policy was applied.

The final general point is that national governments and local authorities will often use a number of policies to achieve the same end. In this case it will be difficult to isolate the results on one of these policies and it would be wise, in many cases, to treat them as a group. For example, the Australian Government supports the dairy industry by a direct grant, by a price equalization scheme, and by restricting the amount of margarine which can be produced. It would be difficult to decide which of these policies encouraged a particular dairy farmer to remain in the industry rather than leave it.

Any geographer concerned with the influence of geographical factors on the operation of policy must deal with the factors which were perceived by the decision-maker and the factors which operate even though they were not perceived. It is often convenient to begin by comparing the obvious results with the announced policy aims, and it was for this reason that the examination of results was made first. There will be two situations. Firstly, if there is a wide disparity between the stated aim and the results three explanations are possible; either perceived factors have operated in an unexpected way, or unperceived factors have operated, or both situations have occurred. For example, if a country with a large wheat surplus tries to discourage production by quotas and incentive payments, yet finds itself with a larger surplus at the end of the year, several explanations may be possible. A remarkably favourable season could have given exceptional yields; farmers may not have co-operated in the manner expected; or marketing problems may have become more acute. Where a policy fails the politician will often identify the unperceived factors for the geographer since they will welcome excuses, and it will often be claimed that such factors were impossible to recognize beforehand.

The second situation will occur when there is a marked correspondence between the aims and results of a particular policy. It is tempting in this case to accept that all factors were perceived, but the danger is that some unperceived factors may have operated in favour of the policy aims. Such situations will not be identified by the politicians concerned! For example, in the case discussed above of a country seeking to reduce a large wheat surplus, if the surplus is reduced the most important factor may have been the failure of a harvest in another part of the world which improved marketing conditions, rather than quotas and incentive payments in the country concerned. The investigation of the operation of geographical factors is appropriate in both contemporary and historical studies, subject to the qualifications mentioned in the discussion about the results of the applications of policies. The greatest difficulty will occur when the policy applies to only a small sector of the economy. For example, the policy to freeze certain rents in British Columbia in 1970, affected many people, and geographers interested in this question should experience little difficulty in obtaining views about the operation of such policies. At the same time policies by the British Columbian Government in respect of timber companies affect only a few very large interests, and opinions about such policies would be difficult to acquire when the policies seemed to favour the large companies.

Conclusion

There are three questions which any political geographer studying policy must face. The first question asks the extent to which political geographers should involve themselves in research into policies. The justification must be that of a scholar seeking knowledge and seeking to apply that knowledge to the resolution of difficulties and problems. Geographers should welcome the opportunity of giving expert opinions about all the stages where geography and public policy intertwine. However, if the political geographer becomes totally committed to a particular policy, which must be based on many factors, such as the use of environment or the deployment of troops in Vietnam, he forfeits any expert standing and has the same rights and importance as any lay critic or proponent.

The second question concerns the extent to which political geographers should focus on particular aspects of policy. There is a need for a concentrated effort, at present, because there are so few political geographers working in this important field. It is therefore suggested that except in the case of historical situations, where there is profuse documentation in archives, geographers should focus on the influence of geographical factors on the operation of policies, and the geographical results which flow from the application of policies. These studies are the easiest to make and therefore will yield the fastest results. Further, if different geographers analysed the same policies, it could be anticipated that their results would be nearly identical in considering the results of policies, and show the greatest divergence in assessing the influence of geographical factors on policy formation. It is also advocated that comparative studies should be made as early as possible. The comparisons could involve similar policies in similar countries; similar policies in different countries; and similar policies at different periods in the same country.

The final question considers what benefits will flow to geography through an increased consideration of government policy at various levels. The first consequence would hopefully be the production of better policies. If geographers are successful in showing how policies may have many unexpected geographical results, and be influenced by unperceived geographical factors, then the knowledge of decision-makers will be improved. This will also lead to an improved status for geography and perhaps increase the funds available for research and the possibility of placing graduates in non-academic positions. Any improved recognition would also attract attention from other disciplines. Many lawyers struggle with concepts of the continental shelf and territorial waters unaware of the work done by geographers; and many economists and historians grapple with the problems of defining regions in complete innocence of the vast geographical literature on the subject. Situations like these owe something to the reluctance of some geographers to publicize their work outside the field, and to consider the practical issues which concern other scholars.

Another important consequence would be that many different kinds of geographers would be involved in the study of policies. The field is of concern to economic geographers, population geographers, urban geographers, historical geographers and geomorphologists. In short, the study of policy will encourage geographers with different specialist interests to talk to each other, and mitigate, to some extent, the present divisive tendencies in the subject.

References

ADEJUYIBGE, O. (1970) Ife–Ijesa boundary problems. *Niger. Geogr. J.* 13, 23–38.

ALEXANDER, L. M. (ed.) (1967) *The Law of the Sea: Off-shore Boundaries and Zones.* Columbus, Ohio.

ALKER, H. R., JR (1964) Dimensions of conflict in the General Assembly. *Am. Pol. Sci. Rev.* 58, 642–57.

ALKER, H. R., JR (1965) *World Politics in the General Assembly.* New Haven.

ALKER, H. R., JR, and RUSSETT, B. M. (1964) On measuring inequality. *Behavioural Sci.* 9, 207–18.

ANDERSON, G. M. (1966) Voting behaviour and the ethnic-religious variable: a study of the election in Hamilton, Ontario. *Can. J. of Econ. and Pol. Sci.* 32, 27–37.

ANDREW, B. H. (1949) Some queries concerning the Texas–Louisiana Sabine boundary. *Southwestern Hist. Q.* 53, 1–18.

BERELSON, B. (1952) *Content Analysis in Communication Research.* New York.

BERGH, G. VAN DEN (1955) *Unity in Diversity.* London.

BERRY, B. J. L. (1964) Approaches to regional analysis: a synthesis. *Ann. Assoc. Am. Geogr.* 54, 2–10.

BERRY, B. J. L. (1969) Review of Russett's *International Regions and the International System. Geogr. Rev.* 59, 450–1.

BILLINGTON, M. (1959) The Red River boundary controversy. *Southwestern Hist. Q.* 62, 356–63.

BIRLEY, E. (1952) *The Congress of Roman Frontier Studies 1949.* Durham.

BLASIER, C. (1966) Power and social change in Colombia: the Cauca valley. *J. of Inter-American Stud.* 8, 366–410.

BLIJ, H. J. DE (1967) *Systematic Political Geography.* New York.

BOGGS, S. W. (1940) *International Boundaries: a Study of Boundary Functions and Problems.* New York.

BOHANNAN, P. and L. (1953) *The Tiv of Central Nigeria.* London.

BOWDEN, J. J. (1959) The Texas–New Mexico boundary dispute along the Rio Grande. *Southwestern Hist. Q.* 63, 221–37.

BRADBURY, R. E. (1957) *The Benin Kingdom.* London.

BRETON, R. J-L. (1968) Partages, réduction, et renovation du Pundjab. *L'information Géographique* 32, 23–36.

BROOKFIELD, H. C. and TATHAM, M. A. (1957) The distribution of racial groups in Durban: the background of apartheid in a South African city. *Geogr. Rev.* 47, 44–65.

BROWN, L. A. (1969) Spatial competition, information flows and opinions: a model. Paper delivered to the annual meeting of the Am. Pol. Sci. Assoc., September, 1969, New York.

BUCKHOLTS, P. (1966) *Political Geography.* New York.

BUNGE, W. (1966) *Theoretical Geography,* Lund studies in Geography, Series C, No. 1.

BUTLER, D. E. and STOKES, D. E. (1969) *Political Change in Britain.* London.

CARTER, F. W. (1969) An analysis of the medieval Serbian Oecumene, a theoretical approach. *Geografiska Ann.* 51B, 39–56.

CATCHPOLE, A. J. W., MOODIE, D. W. and KAYE, B. (1970) Content analysis, a method for the identification of dates of first freezing and first breaking from descriptive accounts. *Prof. Geogr.* 22, 252–7.

CHAPMAN, B. B. (1949) The claims of Texas to Greer County. *Southwestern Hist. Q.* 53, 401–24.

CLARKE, T. D. (1959) *Frontier America.* New York.

COLE, J. P. and KING, C. A. M. (1968) *Quantitative Geography.* London.

COMMONWEALTH OF AUSTRALIA (1968) *Redistribution of the State of Victoria into Electoral Divisions,* Vol. 1. Melbourne.

CORNISH, V. (1923) *The Great Capitals: an Historical Geography.* London.

COX, K. R. (1968) Suburbia and voting behaviour in the London Metropolitan Area. *Ann. Assoc. Am. Geogr.* 58, 111–27.

COX, K. R. (1969) The voting decision in a spatial context, in BOARD, C., CHORLEY, R. J., HAGGETT, P. and STODDART, D. R. (eds) *Progr. in Geogr.* 1. London.

CRONE, G. R. (1967) *Background to Political Geography.* London.

CUKWURAH, A. O. (1967) *The Settlement of Boundary Disputes in International Law.* Manchester.

CURZON OF KEDLESTON, LORD (1907) *Frontiers.* The Romanes Lecture, Oxford.

DAUER, M. J. and KELSAY, R. G. (1955) Unrepresentative states. *Nation. Municipal Rev.* 44, 571–5 and 587.

DAVEAU, S. (1959) *Les régions frontalières de la montagne Jurassienne.* Paris.

DORION, H. (1963) La frontière Québec-Terreneuve. Québec.

DUVERGER, M. (1964) *Introduction to the Social Sciences: with special reference to their methods.* London. Translated by M. Anderson.

EAST, W. G. (1937) The nature of political geography. *Politica* 2, 259–86.

EAST, W. G. (1950) How strong is the heartland? *Foreign Affairs* 29, 78–93.

EAST, W. G. (1960) The geography of landlocked states. *Trans. Inst. Brit. Geogr*, 28, 1–22.

EAST, W. G. (1962) *An Historical Geography of Europe.* 4th edn revised. London.

EAST, W. G. (1968) Political organizations at higher ranks, in FISHER, C. A. (ed.), *Essays in Political Geography.* London.

EMERY, K. O. (1967) Geological aspects of sea-law sovereignty, in ALEXANDER, L. M. (ed.) (1967), Columbus, Ohio.

FAIRGRIEVE, J. (1915) *Geography and World Power.* London.

FARRELL, R. B. (1966) *Approaches to Comparative and International Politics.* Evanston, Illinois.

FAWCETT, C. B. (1918) *Frontiers, a Study in Political Geography.* Oxford.

FESLER, J. W. (1949) *Area and Administration.* Alabama.

FISHER, C. A. (1962) Southeast Asia: the Balkans of the Orient. *Geogr.* 47, 347–67.

FISHER, C. A. (1965) The Vietnamese problem in its geographical context. *Geogr. J.* 131, 502–15.

FISHER, C. A. (1968) The Britain of the East? A study in the geography of imitation. *Mod. Asian Stud.* 2, 343–76.

FOLADARE, I. S. (1968) The effect of neighbourhood on voting behaviour. *Pol. Sci. Q.* 16, 266–72.

FORDE, D. C. and JONES, G. I. (1950) *The Ibo and Ibibio Speaking Peoples of Southeastern Nigeria.* Oxford.

FRIEDHEIM, R. L. (1967) Factor analysis as a tool in studying the law of the sea, in ALEXANDER, L. M. (ed.) (1967), Columbus, Ohio.

FUCKS, W. (1965) *Formeln zur Macht* (Formulae for power). Stuttgart.

GANSER, K. (1966) Socialgeographische Gliederung der Stadt München aufgrund der Verhaltensweisen der Bevolkerung bei politische Wahlen (A division of the city of Munich into social areas by means of voting behaviour of political electors), *Muncher Geographische Hefte* 28.

THE GEOGRAPHER (1970) *Kuwait–Saudi Arabia boundary.* International Boundary Study, 103, Washington.

GERMAN, F. C. (1960) A tentative evaluation of world power. *J. of Conflict Resolution* 4, 138–44.

GIFFORD, P. and LOUIS, W. R. (1967) *Britain and Germany in Africa: Imperial Rivalry and Colonial Rule.* New Haven.

GILBERT, E. W. (1939) Political regionalism in England and Wales. *Geogr. J.* 94, 24–44.

GLANVILLE, T. G. (1970) *Spatial Biases in Electoral Distributions.* Unpubl. thesis, Univ. of Melbourne.

GLENN, N. D. and GRIMES, M. (1968) Ageing, voting and political interest. *Am. Sociol. Rev.* 33, 563–75.

GOGUEL, F. (1951) *Géographie des elections françaises de 1890–1951.* Paris.

GOLDBERG, A. L. (1962) The statistics of malapportionment. *Yale Law J.* 72, 90–101.

GOODEY, B. R. (1968) *The Geography of Elections: an Introductory Bibliography.* Monog. 3, Center for the Study of Cultural and Social Change, Univ. of North Dakota.

GREGORY, S. (1963) *Statistical Methods and the Geographer.* London.

GRIFFITHS, J. A. G. (1965) A new shape for local government. *New Soc.* 6 no. 160, 7–9.

GVELESIANI, G. G. (1965) *Razvitie i razmescenie socialistices kogo proizvodstva v Grunzinsko S.S.R.* (Development and location of socialist productivity in the Georgian S.S.R.). Tbilsi.

GYORGY, A. (1944) *Geopolitics: The New German Science.* Berkeley.

HAMDAN, G. (1963) The political map of new Africa. *Geogr. Rev.* 53, 418–39.

HAMPTON, W. (1968) The electoral response to a multi-vote ballot. *Pol. Stud.* 16, 266–72.

HARTSHORNE, R. (1935) Recent developments in political geography. *Am. Pol. Sci. Rev.* 29, 785–804 and 943–66.

HARTSHORNE, R. (1954) Political geography. Chapter in JAMES, P. E. and JONES C. F. (eds), *American Geography: Inventory and Prospect.* Syracuse.

HARTSHORNE, R. (1950) The Franco-German boundary of 1871. *Wld Politics* 2, 209–50.

HARVEY, D. (1969) *Explanation in Geography.* London.

HELIN, R. A. (1967) The volatile administrative map of Rumania. *Ann. Assoc. Am. Geogr.* 57, 481–502.

HELIN, R. A. (1968) Uniting the wings of Pakistan: a matter of circulation. *Prof. Geogr.* 20, 251–6.

HILL, J. (1965) El Chamizal: a century-old boundary dispute. *Geogr. Rev.* 55, 510–22.

HILL, N. L. (1945) *Claims to Territory in International Law and Relations.* London.

HINKS, A. L. (1940) Review of Bogg's *International Boundaries. Geogr. J.* 96, 286–9.

HITCHNER, D. G. and HARROLD, W. H. (1962) *Modern Government: a Survey of Political Science.* New York.

HODDER, B. W. (1968) The Ewe problem: a reassessment, in FISHER, C. A. (ed.), *Essays in Political Geography.* London.

HUNTINGFORD, C. W. B. (1955) *The Galla of Ethiopia.* London.

HURSTFIELD, J. (1953) *The Control of Raw Materials.* London.

JACKSON, W. A. D. (1964) *Politics and Geographic Relationships.* Englewood Cliffs, N. J.

JAMES, J. R., HOUSE, J. W. and HALL, P. (1970) Local government reform in England: a symposium. *Geogr. J.* 136, 1–23.

JEANS, D. N. (1967) Territorial divisions and the location of towns in New South Wales 1826–42. *Aust. Geogr.* 10, 243–55.

JELAVICH, C. and B. (1965) *The Balkans.* Englewood Cliffs, N.J.

JOHNSON, R. W. (1966) The Canada–United States controversy over the Columbia River. *Univ. of Washington Law Rev.* 41, 676–763.

JONES, S. B. (1945) *Boundary making, a Handbook for Statesmen.* Washington.

JONES, S. B. (1954) A unified field theory of political geography. *Ann. Assoc. Am. Geogr.* 44, 111–23.

JONES, S. B. (1959) Global strategic views, in *Military Aspects of World Political Geography.* Alabama.

KAISER, H. F. (1968) A measure of the quality of legislative apportionment. *Am. Pol. Sci. Rev.* 62, 208–15.

KAPIL, R. L. (1968) Political boundaries and territorial instability. *Internat. Rev. of Hist. and Pol. Sci.* 5, 46–78.

KARAN, P. P. (1966) The India–Pakistan enclave problem. *Prof. Geogr.* 18, 23–5.

KASPERSON, R. E. and MINGHI, J. V. (1969) *The Structure of Political Geography.* Chicago.

KELLY, K. (1969) An explanation of the great north–south extent of the Inca Empire in 1532, and of the position of its eastern boundary through Peru and Bolivia. *J. of Trop. Geogr.* 28, 57–63.

KIBULYA, H. M. and LANGLANDS, B. W. (1967) *The Political Geography of the Uganda–Congo Boundary.* Makerere University College.

KINNEAR, M. (1968) *The British Voter.* London.

KLEBER, L. C. (1968) The Mason–Dixon Line. *Hist. Today* 18, 117–23.

KRIPPENDORFF, E. (1966) A critique of Bonn's Ostpolitik. *Survey* 61, 47–55.

KRISTOF, L. K. D. (1959) The nature of frontiers and boundaries. *Ann. Assoc. Am. Geogr.* 49, 269–82.

KRISTOF, L. K. D. (1960) The origins and evolution of geopolitics. *J. of Conflict Resolutions* 4, 15–51.

LAKEMAN, E. (1970) *How Democracies Vote.* London.

LAMB, A. (1966) *The McMahon Line.* 2 vols. London.

LAPRADELLE, P. DE (1928) *La Frontière: étude de droit international.* Paris.

LASSWELL, H. D. and LEITES, N. (1949) *Language of Politics.* New York.

LATTIMORE, O. (1962) *Studies in Frontier History.* London.

LEWIS, P. E. (1965) Impact of Negro Migration on the electoral geography of Flint, Michigan 1932–62; a cartographic analysis. *Ann. Assoc. Am. Geogr.* 55, 1–25.

LEWIS, P. W. and SKIPWORTH, G. E. (1966) *Some geographical and statistical aspects of the distribution of votes in recent general elections.* Hull.

LIPMAN, V. D. (1949) *Local Government Areas 1843–45.* Oxford.

LÖSCH, A. (1954) *The Economics of Location,* translated by W. H. Woglom and W. F. Stolper. New Haven.

LOWI, T. J. (1964) American business, public policy case studies and political theory. *Wld Pol.* 16, 677–715.

MCCOLL, R. W. (1966) Political geography as political ecology. *Prof. Geogr.* 18, 143–5.

MCCOLL, R. W. (1967) A political geography of revolutionary China, Vietnam and Thailand. *J. of Conflict Resolution* 21, 153–67.

MCCOLL, R. W. (1969) The insurgent state: territorial bases of revolution. *Ann. Assoc. Am. Geogr.* 59, 613–31.

MACKAY, J. R. (1958) The interactance hypothesis and boundaries in Canada: a preliminary study. *Can. Geogr.* 11, 1–8.

MACKENZIE, W. J. M. (1958) *Free Elections.* London.

MCPHAIL, I. R. (1970) Characteristics of the vote for Mayor – Los Angeles, 1969. Paper presented to the 42nd Congr. of Aust. and N.Z. Assoc. for the Adv. of Sci. Port Moresby.

MARSHALL-CORNWALL, J. H. (1935) *Geographic Disarmament: a Study in Regional Demilitarization.* London.

MELAMID, A. (1957) The political geography of the Gulf of Aquaba. *Ann. Assoc. Am. Geogr.* 47, 231–40.

MELAMID, A. (1968) The Shatt el–Arab boundary dispute. *The Middle E. J.* 22, 351–7.

MICHAELS, D. W. (1966) Review of Fucks' *Formeln zur Macht. Prof. Geogr.* 18, 305–10.

MINISTÈRE DES COLONIES (1910) *Documents scientifiques de la mission Tilho.* Paris.

MONKHOUSE, F. J. and WILKINSON, H. R. (1971) *Maps and Diagrams: their compilation and construction.* 3rd edn. London.

MOODIE, E. A. (1956) *The Geography behind Politics.* London.

MORTON, W. L. (1965) The geographical circumstances of confederation. *Can. Geogr. J.* 70, 74–87.

MOSELEY, G. (1965) China's fresh approach to the national minority question. *The China Q.* 24, 15–27.

MOSER, C. A. (1958) *Survey Methods in Social Investigation.* London.

MULLER-WILLE, W. (1966) Politisch-geographische Leitbilder, reale Lebensraume und global Spanningsfolder (Leading ideas in political geography, the realities of populated space and global fields of tension). *Geographische Zeits.* 54, 13–38.

NACHTIGAL, G. (1879) *Sahara und Sudan*. Berlin.

NATIONAL ACADEMY OF SCIENCES – NATIONAL RESEARCH COUNCIL (1965) *The Science of Geography*, publ. 1277, Washington, D.C.

NICHOLSON, N. L. (1954) *The Boundaries of Canada: its Provinces and Territories*. Dept. of Mines and Technical Surveys, Geological Branch, Memoir 2, Ottawa.

NOOIJ, A. T. J. (1969) Political radicalism among Dutch Farmers. *Sociologia Ruralis* 9, 43–61.

OLIVER, R. and ATMORE, A. (1967) *Africa since 1800*. Cambridge.

ORR, D. (1969) The persistence of gerrymandering in North Carolina redistricting. *South Eastern Geogr.* 9, 39–54.

PADELFORD, N. J. and LINCOLN, G. A. (1954) *International Politics*. New York.

PALLIS, A. A. (1925) Racial migrations in the Balkans during the years 1912–24. *Geogr. J.* 66, 315–31.

PAULLIN, C. O. (1932) *Atlas of the Historical Geography of the United States*. Washington.

PELLING, H. (1967) *The Social Geography of British Elections 1885–1910*. London.

PERHAM, M. and BULL, M. (1962) *The Diaries of Lugard*. Vol. 4. London.

POUNDS, N. J. G. (1963) *Political Geography*. New York.

POUNDS, N. J. G. (1964) History and geography: a perspective on partition. *J. of Internat. Affairs* 18, 161–72.

PRESCOTT, J. R. V. (1959) The function and methods of electoral geography. *Ann. Assoc. Am. Geogr.* 49, 296–304.

PRESCOTT, J. R. V. (1959b) Les régions politiques des Camerouns Anglo-Français. *Ann. de Géogr.* 263–7.

PRESCOTT, J. R. V. (1965) *The Geography of Frontiers and Boundaries*. London.

PRESCOTT, J. R. V. (1966) Resources, policy and development in West and North Central Africa, in HOUSE, J. W. (ed.), *Northern Geographical Essays*. Newcastle upon Tyne.

PRESCOTT, J. R. V. (1968) *The Geography of State Policies*. London.

PRESCOTT, J. R. V. (1970) Electoral studies in political geography, in KASPERSON, R. E. and MINGHI, J. V. (eds), *The Structure of Political Geography*. Chicago.

RAISZ, E. (1948) *General Cartography*. New York.

RANTALA, O. (1967) Political regions of Finland. *Scandinavian Pol. Stud.* 2, 117–40.

REYNOLDS, D. R. and ARCHER, J. C. (1969) An inquiry into the spatial basis of electoral geography. *Discuss. Pap. 11*. Univ. of Iowa.

REYNOLDS, D. R. and MCNULTY, M. L. (1968) On the analysis of political boundaries as barriers: a perceptual approach. *East Lakes Geogr.* 4, 21–38.

REYNOLDS, D. R. (1969) Spatial dimensions of electoral behaviour: some theoretical and methodical considerations, paper delivered to 65th Annual Meeting of the Am. Pol. Sci. Assoc. New York.

RICHARDS, P. G. (1965) Local government reform: smaller towns and the countryside. *Urb. Stud.* 2, 147–62.

RICHMOND, I. A. (1966) *Handbook to the Roman Wall*. London.

RILEY, R. C. (1965) Recent developments in the Belgian Borinage: an area of declining coal production in the European Coal and Steel Community. *Geogr.* 50, 261–73.

ROBERTS, M. C. and RUMAGE, K. W. (1965) The spatial variations in urban left-wing voting in England and Wales, 1951. *Ann. Assoc. Am. Geogr.* 55, 161–78.

ROBINSON, K. W. (1961) Sixty years of federation in Australia. *Geogr. Rev.* 51, 1–20.

ROBINSON, K. W. (1962) Political influence in Australian geography. *Pac. Viewp.* 3, 73–86.

ROBSON, W. A. (ed.) (1954) *The University Teaching of Social Sciences: Political Science*. UNESCO, Paris.

ROOS, L. J. (1969) Development *versus* distribution: an attitudinal study of Turkish local administration. *J. of Econ. Dev. and Cult. Change* 17, 552–66.

ROSE, A. J. (1966) *Dilemmas down under*. New Jersey.

ROSENAU, J. N. (ed.) (1969) *Linkage Politics: Essays on the Convergence of National and International Systems*. New York.

RUSSETT, B. M. (1966) Discovering voting groups in the United Nations. *Amer. Pol. Sci. Rev.* 60, 327–39.

RUSSETT, B. M. (1967) *International Regions and the International Systems*. Chicago.

SCHAT, P. (1969) Political geography: a review. *Tidjschr. Econ. Soc. Geogr.* 60, 255–60.

SCHOLLER, P. (1957) Wege und irrwege der Politischen Geographie und Geopolitic (Advances and abberrations of political geography and geopolitics). *Erdk.* 11, 1–20.

SCHUTZ, W. (1950) *Theory and Methodology of Content Analysis*. New York.

SCHWEINFURTH, U. (1965) Der Himalayer-Landschaftscheide, Ruckzugsgebeit und politisches Spanningsfeld (The Himalayas – divider of landscape, region of withdrawal and zone of political tension). *Geogr. Zeits.* 53, 241–60.

SCOTT, P. (1955) Cape Town: a multi-racial city. *Geogr. J.* 121, 149–57.

SEVIAN, V. J. (1968) The evolution of the boundary between Iran and Iraq, in FISHER, C. A. (ed.) *Essays in Political Geography*, London.

SEVRIN, R. (1949) Les échanges de population à la frontière entre la France et la Tournaisis. *Ann. de Geogr.* 58, 237–44.

SEWELL, W. R. D. (1968) The role of attitudes of engineers in water management, in STRODTBEK, F. L. and WHITE, G. F. (eds). *Attitudes towards water: an inter-disciplinary exploration*. Chicago.

SHAWCROSS, LORD (1967) The law of the continental shelf with special references to the North Sea. *Congr. Proc. 20th Internat. Geogr. Congr.* 77–84.

SIEGFRIED, A. (1938) Foreword in Ancel J. *Les frontières*. Paris.

SIEGFRIED, A. (1947) *Géographie electorale de l'Ardèche*. Paris.

SMITH, B. (1965) *Regionalism in England: 2. Its nature and purpose, 1905–65*. London.

SMITH, H. R. and HART, J. F. (1955) The American tariff map. *Geogr. Rev.* 45, 327–46.

SOJA, E. W. (1968) Communication and territorial integration in East Africa. *East Lakes Geogr.* 4, 39–57.

SOLWAY, P. (1965) *The Frontier Peoples of Roman Britain*. London.

SPATE, O. H. K. (1942) Factors in the development of capital cities. *Geogr. Rev.* 22, 622–31.

SPATE, O. H. K. (1967) *India and Pakistan*. 3rd edn., London, 1967.

SPROUT, H. H. (1968) Political geography, in *International Encyclopedia of the Social Sciences* 6, New York.

SPYKMAN, N. J. (1933) Methods of approach to the study of international relations. *Proc. 5th Conf. of Internat. Law and Related Subjects* 60–9, Washington.

STANLEY, D. R. (1968) *The Geography of New South Wales Elections 1932–1965*. Unpubl. thesis, Univ. of Melbourne.

STEPHENSON, G. V. (1968) Pakistan's discontiguity and the majority problem. *Geogr. Rev.* 58, 195–213.

STEVENSON, R. F. (1968) *Population and Political Systems in Tropical Africa*, New York.

TAYLOR, P. J. (1971) *Bibliography of Political Redistribution – First Draft*. Univ. of Iowa.

TILHO (1910) *Documents scientifiques de la mission Tilho*. Ministère des Colonies. Paris.

TURNER, F. J. (1953) *The Frontier in American History*. 3rd imp. New York.

WALLACE, M. D. (1969) Power, states and interstate wars. Paper presented to the 41st annual meeting of the Can. Pol. Sci. Assoc., York University.

WATT, W. M. (1966) The political relevance of Islam in East Africa. *Internat. Affairs* 42, 35–44.

WEIGERT, H. W. (1957) *Principles of Political Geography*. New York.

WIENS, H. J. (1969) Changes in the ethnology and land-use of the Ili valley and region of Chinese Turkestan, *Ann. Assoc. Am. Geogr.* 59, 753–75.

WITTHUHN, B. O. (1968) The spatial integration of Uganda as shown by the diffusion of postal agencies, 1900–1965. *East Lakes Geogr.* 4, 5–20.

WOLFE, R. I. (1963) *Transportation and Politics*. Princeton.

WOLPERT, J. (1965) Behavoural aspects of the decision to migrate. *Pap. Reg. Sci. Assoc.* 15, 159–69.

WOOLMINGTON, E. R. (1966) *A spatial approach to the measurement of support for the separatist movement in Northern New South Wales*. Univ. of New England, Monog. Ser., no. 2 Armidale.

WOOSTER, R. A. (1962) *The Secessionist Conventions of the South*. New Jersey.

WRIGHT, J. K. (1944) Training for research in political geography. *Ann. Assoc. Am. Geogr.* 34, 190–201.

WRIGHT, Q. (1955) *The Study of International Relations*. New York.

YOUNG, O. R. (1969) Professor Russett: industrious tailor to a naked emperor. *Wld Pol.* 21, 486–511.

YOUNG, P. V. (1956) *Scientific Social Surveys and Research*. New York.

ZARTMAN, L. W. (1965) The politics of boundaries in north and west Africa. *J. Mod. Afr. Stud.* 3, 155–73.

ZIMMERMAN, H. and KLINGEMANN, H. D. (1967) Der Einfluss der Verteidingungskaufe auf die Regional-struktur in der Bundesrepublik Deutschland (The influence of defence buying regional structure in the Federal Republic of Germany). *Raumforschung und Raumordnung* 25, 49–60.

ZWANZIG, G. W. (1965) Das Landespflagerecht in Mittel-europa (The law of land conservation in Central Europe). *Die Erde* 96, 301–3.

Appendix

The metric system: conversion factors and symbols

In common with several other textbook series *The Field of Geography* uses the metric units of measurement recommended for scientific journals by the Royal Society Conference of Editors.* For geography texts the most commonly used of these units are:

Physical quantity	Name of unit	Symbol for unit	Definition of non-basic units
length	metre	m	basic
area	square metre	m²	basic
	hectare	ha	$10^4\,\mathrm{m}^2$
mass	kilogramme	kg	basic
	tonne	t	$10^3\,\mathrm{kg}$
volume	cubic metre	m³	basic-derived
	litre	l	$10^{-3}\,\mathrm{m}^3$, $1\,\mathrm{dm}^3$
time	second	s	basic
force	newton	N	$\mathrm{kg\ m\ s^{-2}}$
pressure	bar	bar	$10^5\,\mathrm{Nm^{-2}}$
energy	joule	J	$\mathrm{kgm^2\,s^{-2}}$
power	watt	W	$\mathrm{kgm^2\,s^{-3}} = \mathrm{Js^{-1}}$
thermodynamic temperature	degree Kelvin	°K	basic
customary temperature, t	degree Celsius	°C	$t\,/°\mathrm{C} = T\,/°\mathrm{K} - 273{\cdot}15$

Fractions and multiples

Fraction	Prefix	Symbol	Multiple	Prefix	Symbol
10^{-1}	deci	d	10	deka	da
10^{-2}	centi	c	10^2	hecto	h
10^{-3}	milli	m	10^3	kilo	k
10^{-6}	micro	μ	10^6	mega	M

The gramme (g) is used in association with numerical prefixes to avoid such absurdities as mkg for μg or kkg for Mg.

* Royal Society Conference of Editors, *Metrication in Scientific Journals*, London, 1968.

Conversion of common British units to metric units

Length

1 mile   1·609 km
1 furlong = 0·210 km
1 chain   = 20·117 m

1 fathom = 1·829 m
1 yard   = 0·914 m
1 foot   = 0·305 m
1 inch   = 25·4 mm

Area

1 sq mile = 2·590 km²
1 acre   = 0·405 ha

1 sq foot = 0·093 m²
1 sq inch = 645·16 mm²

Mass

1 ton   = 1·016 t
1 cwt   = 50·802 kg
1 stone = 6·350 kg

1 lb = 0·454 kg
1 oz = 28·350 g

Mass per unit length and per unit area

1 ton/mile = 0·631 t/km
1 lb/ft   = 1·488 kg/m

1 ton/sq mile = 392·298 kg/km²
1 cwt/acre   = 125·535 kg/ha

Volume and capacity

1 cubic foot = 0·028 m³
1 cubic inch = 1638·71 mm³
I US barrel = 0·159 m³
1 bushel   = 0·036 m³

1 gallon   = 4·546 l
1 US gallon = 3·785 l
1 quart   = 1·137 l
1 pint   = 0·568 l
1 gill   = 0·142 l

Velocity

1 m.p.h. = 1·609 km/h
1 ft/s   = 0·305 m/s

1 UK knot = 1·853 km/h

Mass carried × distance

1 ton mile = 1·635 t km

Force

1 ton-force = 9·964 kN
1 lb-force = 4·448 N

1 poundal = 0·138 N
1 dyn   = 10⁻⁵ N

Pressure

1 ton-force/ft² = 107·252 kN/m²
1 lb-force/in² = 68·948 mbar

1 pdl/ft² = 1·488 N/m²

Energy and power

1 therm	= 105·506 MJ	1 Btu	= 1·055 kJ
1 hp	= 745·700 W(J/s)	1 ft lb-force	= 1·356 J
	= 0·746 kW	1 ft pdl	= 0·042 J
1 hp/hour	= 2·685 MJ	1 cal	= 4·187 J
1 kWh	= 3·6 MJ	1 erg	= 10^{-7} J

Metric units have been used in the text wherever possible. British or other standard equivalents have been added in brackets in a few cases where metric units are still only used infrequently by English-speaking readers.

Index

Adejuyigbe, O., 71, 105
Administrative actions and decisions, 16, 17, 18, 19, 20, 21, 22, 23
Alexander, L. M., 20, 105
Alker, H. R. Jr, 48, 105
Alker, H. R. Jr and Russett, B. M., 80, 105
Alliances, 13
Analytical political geography, 2, 14
Anderson, G. M., 11, 105
Andrew, B. H., 67, 105
Annexation, 59
Archer, J. C. and Reynolds, D. R., 84, 85, 86, 87, 111
Aristotle, 7
Atmore, A. and Oliver, R., 59, 111

Bascom, W., 20
Berelson, B., 33, 105
Berry, B. J. L., 6, 40, 105
Bilateral agreements, 16
Billington, M., 61, 105
Birley, E., 55, 105
Blasier, C., 11, 105
Blij, H. J. de, 9, 13, 27, 51, 105
Bodin, J., 7
Boggs, S. W., 41, 105
Bohannan, P. and L., 57, 105
Border regulations, 73
Boundaries, 54–74
    aspects of interest to political geographers, 55
    behavioural study of, 55–6, 61–74
    classification of, 35
    electoral, 10, 81, 82
    evolution of, 55, 63–6
    geographers' contribution to study of, 55
    influence on individual behaviour, 55, 61
    influence on landscape, 55
    influence on state policies and development, 55

internal, 22, 25, 61, 63, 71
international, 22, 25, 61, 63–6
mathematical analysis of, 41–4 fig.
position of, 55, 63–4
state functions at, 72
systematic study of, 55, 61
Boundary disputes, 12, 13, 66–72
    factors influencing outcome of, 67–9
    functional, 66, 72
    geographical arguments in, 69–70, 71
    geographical results of, 71–2
    non-geographical arguments in, 69, 71
    positional, 66, 67, 68, 71
    resource, 66, 68, 72
    sub-national, 67
    territorial, 13, 66, 68, 69
    types of, 66
Bowden, J. J., 67, 105
Bradbury, R. E., 57, 105
Breton, R. J. L., 20, 106
Brookfield, H. C. and Tatham, M. A., 10, 106
Brown, L. A., 6, 84, 106
Buchanan, K. M., 51
Buckholts, P., 1, 106
Buffer states, 22, 59
Bull, M. and Perham, M., 65, 111
Burgh, P. van den, 81
Burghardt, A., 84
Butler, D. E. and Stokes, D. E., 30, 86, 106

Carter, F. W., 49, 50, 106
Cartographic analysis, 36–8
Catchpole, A. J. W., Moodie, D. W. and Kaye, B., 33, 106
Chapman, B. B., 20, 67, 106
Christy, F. T. C., 20
Clarke, T. D., 61, 106
Classical analysis, 32, 36, 38–9
Classification in geography, 35

Cognitive behaviourism, 38
Cole, J. R. and King, C. A. M., 40, 106
Colonization,
    studies by geographers, 12
    studies by political scientists, 11–12
Commercial pressure groups, 14, 15 fig.,
    16, 24
Comparative analysis, 34, 36, 39, 51
Comparative political geography, need
    for, 103
Constitutions, aspects relevant to geo-
    graphy, 5 fig., 7–8
Content analysis, 33
Cornish, V., 9, 106
Cox, K. R., 84, 85, 86, 88, 89, 106
Crone, G. R., 4, 106
Cukwurah, A. O., 69, 106
Curzon of Kedleston, Lord, 59, 106

Dauer, M. J. and Kelsay, R. G., 79, 106
Dauer–Kelsay index of representative-
    ness, 79–80
Daveau, S., 73, 106
Decision-makers, 14, 98, 103
Defence actions and decisions, 16, 17,
    19, 20, 21, 22, 23
Descriptive political geography, 2, 3
Development actions and decisions,
    16, 17, 18, 19, 20, 21, 23
Development policies,
    general multilaterial, 97
    general unilaterial, 97
    specific multilateral, 97
    specific unilateral, 97
Dorion, H., 41, 61, 106
Duverger, M., 30, 32, 106

East, W. G., 2, 12, 13, 59, 90, 106, 107
Economic functions of states, 9–10
Economic patterns, effect of political
    actions and decisions on, 15 fig.,
    20–2
Elections,
    geographical study of, 75–90
    voting patterns, 75, 80–3
Electoral boundaries, 10, 81, 82
Electoral geography, 3, 4–5, 8, 10,
    75–91
    aspects studied by geographers,
    10–11, 75
    mathematical techniques in, 47, 51,
    85–7, 88
    studies on, 11, 36

Electoral system,
    description of geographical char-
    acteristics, 75–81
    geographical explanation of, 10,
    83–9
Electorates, drawing of, 83–4
Emery, K. O., 13, 107

Factor analysis, 48, 49
Farrell, R. B., 4, 107
Fawcett, C. B., 70, 107
Federations, 8, 18, 21
Fesler, J. W., 9, 107
Fisher, C. A., 2, 39, 90, 107
Fishing, control of coastal waters, 48
Foladare, I. S., 85, 107
Forde, D. C. and Jones, G. I., 57, 107
Foreign policy, significance of factors
    in, 39, 49
Friedheim, R. L., 11, 48, 49, 90, 107
Frontiers, 54–74
    behavioural analysis, 58–61
    political, 56–60
    political features of, 57
    primary settlement, 56–8, 60–1
    secondary settlement, 56
    studies on, 57, 60, 61
    systematic study of, 56–8
Fucks, W., 45, 46, 107

Ganser, K., 11, 107
Geographer, The, 2, 64
Geographical factors,
    classification of, 4, 5 fig.
    influence on boundary evolution,
    64–5
    influence on individual actions, 62
    influence on policies, 62, 97–103
    influence on politics, 2–14, 5 fig.
Geographical patterns,
    influence of political actions and
    decisions on, 3, 14–26, 15 fig.
German, F. L., 45, 107
Gerrymandering,
    types of, 76–7
    tests to determine, 77, 78 fig., 79 fig.
Gifford, D. and Louis, W. R., 13, 107
Gilbert, E. W., 9, 107
Glanville, T. G., 76, 107
Glenn, N. D. and Grimes, M., 86, 108
Goguel, P., 6, 53, 84, 108
Goldberg, A. L., 80, 108
Goodey, B. R., 84, 108

Governments, classification of functions, 15 fig., 16
Government regulations, effect on physical landscape, 23–4
Gregory, S., 40, 108
Griffiths, J. A. G., 9, 107
Grimes, M. and Glenn, N. D., 86, 108
Gvelesiani, G. G., 20, 108

Hall, P., House, J. W. and James, J. R., 9, 109
Hamdan, G., 41, 108
Hampton, W., 89, 108
Harbold, W. H. and Hitchner, D. G., 6, 108
Hart, J. F. and Smith, H. R., 11, 113
Hartshorne, R., 1, 35, 65, 71, 108
Harvey, D., 35, 108
Helin, R. A., 23, 39, 108
Hill, J., 64, 108
Hill, N. L., 69, 108
Hinks, A. L., 41, 108
Historical political geography, 30, 34, 36, 38
Hitchner, D. G. and Harbold, W. H., 6, 108
Hodder, B. W., 72, 108
Holt, R. T. and Turner, J. E., 4, 12, 14
Hoover, E., 51
House, J. W., Hall, P. and James, J. R., 9, 109
Hugonnier, S., 84
Huntingford, C. W. B., 57, 58, 108
Hurstfield, J., 22, 106

Individuals, the need to study their behaviour, 55, 56, 59–60, 61, 62, 72, 74
International assemblies, geographical study of voting in, 90–1
International Monetary Fund, 21
International trade, 21–2, 25
International Wheat Agreement, 21
Island states, 4

Jackson, W. A. D., 1, 109
James, J. R., House, J. W. and Hall, P., 9, 109
Jeans, D. N., 9, 109
Jelavich, B. and C., 12, 109
Johnson, R. W., 13, 109
Jones, G. I. and Forde, D. C., 57, 109
Jones, S. B., 2, 3, 61, 63, 109

Kaiser, H. F., 80, 109
Kapil, R. L., 55, 109
Karan, P. P., 13, 109
Kasperson, R. E. and Minghi, J. V., 1, 9, 33, 109
Kasperson, X., 33
Kaye, B., Catchpole, A. J. W. and Moodie, D. W., 33, 106
Kelly, K., 59, 109
Kelsay, R. G. and Dauer, M. J., 79, 106
Kibulya, H. M. and Langlands, B. W., 51, 73, 109
King, C. A. M. and Cole, J. R., 40, 106
Kinnear, M., 81, 109
Kleber, L. C., 64, 109
Klingemann, H. D. and Zimmerman, H., 21, 114
Krebheil, E., 84
Krippendorf, E., 13, 109
Kristof, L. K. D., 2, 3, 60, 109

Lakeman, E., 81, 109
Lamb, A., 38, 109
Land control, 8
Landlocked states, 12, 48
Langlands, B. W. and Kibulya, H. M., 51, 73, 109
Lapradelle, P. de, 63, 109
Laswell, H. D. and Leites, N., 33, 109
Lattimore, O., 59, 60, 109
Law of the sea, 13, 20
Leites, N. and Laswell, H. D., 33, 109
Lewis, P. E., 35, 37, 88, 110
Lewis, P. W. and Skipworth, G. E., 82, 110
Linkage politics, 4, 5 fig., 12
Lipman, V. D., 9, 110
Local government, 8–9, 18, 19
Lösch, A., 51, 72, 110
Louis, W. R. and Gifford, P., 13, 107
Lowi, T. J., 95, 110

McColl, R. W., 2, 26, 92, 110
McGee, T. G, 51
Mackay, J. R., 41, 72, 110
Mackenzie, W. J. M., 81, 110
Mackinder, H. J., 13
McNulty, M. L. and Reynolds, D. R., 43, 45, 62, 74, 112
McPhail, I. R., 48, 88, 110
Marches, 59
Marshall-Cornwall, J. H., 59, 110

Mathematical analysis, 36, 38, 40–53
  applied to boundary studies, 41–4 fig.
  applied to electoral studies, 42–4 fig.
  measurement of state characteristics, 41–3, 51
  problems associated with, 50–3
  topics suitable for analysis, 41, 44 fig.
  topics unsuitable for analysis, 41, 44 fig., 45, 50
Melamid, A., 13, 67, 110
Merritt, R. K., 4, 12
Michaels, D. W., 40, 110
Military geography, 26
Minghi, J. V. and Kasperson, R. E., 1, 9, 33, 109
Minorities, 13, 83
Models, 40, 41
Monkhouse, F. J. and Wilkinson, H. R., 35, 110
Moodie, D. W., Catchpole, A. J. W. and Kaye, B., 33, 106
Moodie, E. A., 4, 110
Morton, W. L., 8, 110
Moseley, G., 20, 110
Moser, C. A., 30, 110
Muller-Wille, W., 13, 110

Nachtigal, G., 57, 111
National assemblies, geographical study of voting in, 90–1
National capital, 42, 44
National administrative actions, 19, 20, 22
National administrative decisions, 15 fig., 17, 18
National defensive actions, 19, 22, 23
National defence decisions, 15 fig., 17–18, 21
National development actions, 19, 20, 22, 23
National development decisions, 15 fig., 17, 19, 20, 22, 2 3
Neutral zones, 64
Nicholson, N. L., 38, 111
Non-government groups, 16, 24–5
Nooij, A. T. J., 11, 111

Oil companies, policies of interest to political geographers, 92
Oliver, R. and Atmore, A., 59, 111
Orr, D., 76, 111

Pallis, A. A., 16, 111
Partition, 12
Paullin, C. O., 90, 111
Pelling, H., 11, 53, 84, 111
Perham, M. and Bull, M., 65, 111
Physical landscape, influence on political actions, 23
Plebiscites, geographical study of, 75–90
Policy-making, 98–102
Political actions, influence on geographical patterns, 1, 2, 3, 14–26
Political aims, 62, 64
Political decisions, influence on geographical patterns, 1, 2, 3, 14–26
Political geography,
  content of, 2–26
  fieldwork, 28, 29–30, 34, 38, 46
  information sources, 29–34
  methods, 27–53
  objectivity in, 27–8, 32
Political science,
  content, 3–4, 5 fig.
  problems, 6
  awareness of geographical factors, 11
  contributions to political geography, 14
Politics,
  aspects where geography has no relevance, 7
  aspects where geography is relevant, 7–14
  relationships with geography, 3–14, 5 fig.
Population distribution,
  as a geographical factor in politics, 8, 9
  influence of political processes on, 16–19
Pounds, N. J. G., 1, 9, 12, 27, 70, 77, 111
Prescott, J. R. V., 1, 4, 9, 16, 17, 20, 26, 34, 55, 61, 71, 72, 76, 80, 81, 82, 93, 96, 111
Primary sources, 31–3, 38
Public policies, 97–103
  administrative, 96, 97
  aspects of study of, 93–5
  classification of, 95–7
  defence, 96
  definition of, 92–3
  development, 96–7

Public policies – *contd.*
  geographical results of application, 100–1, 102
  methods of analysis, 93, 95–7, 99–100
  problems in analysis of, 98–9, 101–2
  qualities of, 95
  stages at which geography may be significant, 97 fig, 98
  tests to determine types to be considered, 94–5

Qualitative geography, 52–3

Raisz, E., 35, 111
Rantala, O., 85, 111
Rebels, 14, 24
Regional political geography, 2, 8–9, 90–1
Reynolds, D. R., 6, 112
Reynolds, D. R. and Archer, J. C., 84, 85, 86, 87, 111
Reynolds, D. R. and McNulty, M. L., 43, 45, 62, 74, 111
Richards, P. G., 9, 112
Richmond, I. A., 57, 112
Riley, R. C., 18, 112
Roberts, M. C. and Rumage, K. W., 88, 112
Robinson, K. W., 8, 112
Robson, W. A., 3–4, 112
Roos, L. J., 47, 112
Rose, A. J., 12, 112
Rosenau, J. N., 4, 12, 112
Rumage, K. W. and Roberts, M. C., 88, 112
Russett, B. M., 11, 13, 40, 48, 49, 90, 112
Russett, B. M. and Alker, H. J. Jr, 80, 105

Schat, P., 4, 112
Schutz, W., 33, 112
Schweinfurth, U., 7, 112
Scott, P., 10, 112
Secessionist movements, 13, 16, 22, 25–26
Secondary sources, 31, 33, 34
Settlement patterns, effect of political actions and decisions on, 19
Sevian, V. J., 67, 113
Sevrin, R., 73, 113
Sewell, W. R. D., 46, 113

Shawcross, Lord, 13, 113
Siegfried, A., 6, 54, 84, 113
Shipworth, G. E. and Lewis, P. W., 82, 110
Smith, B., 9, 113
Smith, H. R. and Hart J. F., 11, 113
Soja, E. W., 43, 50, 113
Solway, P., 57, 113
Sovereignty over sea-bed, 13
Spate, O. H. K., 2, 9, 38, 51, 90, 113
Spheres of interest and influence, 59
Sprout, H. H., 3, 113
Spykman, N. J., 39, 113
Stanley, D. R., 81, 82, 113
State behaviour, 55, 58–74
  towards frontier inhabitants, 61
  towards neighbouring states, 60–1, 62, 63, 66, 72
State functions at boundaries, 72
States, classification of, 44
Stephenson, G. V., 20, 113
Stevenson, R. F., 8, 113
Stokes, D. E. and Butler, D. E., 30, 86, 106
Sub-national administrative actions, influence on territorial patterns of authority, 22
Sub-national decisions, geographical significance, 15 fig., 16, 18
Sub-national development actions, 20, 21, 22, 23
Supra-national actions
  administrative, 18, 20, 21, 22, 23
  defence, 22, 23
  development, 21, 22, 23
  influence on population patterns, 15 fig., 17
Supra-national decisions, 15 fig.
  administrative, 17, 18, 20, 21
  defence, 22
  development, 21

Tatham, M. A. and Brookfield, H. C., 10, 106
Taylor, P. J., 76, 113
Territorial patterns of authority, 22
Tilho, M., 58, 113
Trade disagreements, 13
Trade patterns, 15 fig.
Trade unions, 14, 15 fig. 24
Transport patterns, 23–4
Turner, J. E. and Holt, R. T., 4, 12, 14
Turner, F. J., 4, 12, 14, 61, 113

Undersea mining, 20
United Nations, 22, 23
Uti possidetis, 69

Votes, *see also* Plebiscites,
  analysis of, 84–90
  discrepancies in patterns of, 88–9
  grouping of, 47, 48
  in international and national assemblies, 90–1
  methods of counting, 81
  patterns of, 10–11, 47–8, 49, 86

Wallace, M. D., 47, 113
Watt, W. M., 12, 114
Weigert, H. W., 3, 114
Weighting, 77–80, 83

Wiens, H. J., 60, 114
Wilkinson, H. R. and Monkhouse, F. J., 35, 110
Witthuhn, B. O., 50, 114
Wolfe, R. I., 23, 114
Wolpert, J., 74, 114
Woolmington, E. R., 11, 37, 93, 114
Wooster, R. A., 97, 114
Wright, J. K., 26, 27, 84, 114

Young, O. R., 40, 49, 114
Young, P. V., 30, 114

Zartman, L. W., 12, 114
Zimmerman, H. and Klingemann, H. D., 21, 114
Zwanzig, G. W., 20, 114

DATE DUE